Samuel Wayland Kershaw

Protestants from France in Their English Home

Samuel Wayland Kershaw

Protestants from France in Their English Home

ISBN/EAN: 9783744649124

Printed in Europe, USA, Canada, Australia, Japan

Cover: Foto ©ninafisch / pixelio.de

More available books at **www.hansebooks.com**

PROTESTANTS FROM FRANCE,

IN THEIR

ENGLISH HOME.

BY

S. W. KERSHAW, F.S.A.

"They maintained their faith in the noble way of persecution, and served God in the fire, whereas we honour Him in the sunshine."
SIR THOMAS BROWNE.

WITH ILLUSTRATIONS.

London:
SAMPSON LOW, MARSTON, SEARLE, & RIVINGTON
CROWN BUILDINGS, 188, FLEET STREET.
1885.

[*All rights reserved.*]

PREFACE.

THE advent and settlement of the Refugees has always formed a part of history; of those who escaped from the dire persecutions in France, much has been written, and yet the subject is not exhausted.

It is the object of this work to chronicle the lives and progress of the fugitives in England, the efforts which aided and the influences that guided their course, especially in relation to the English Church.

To illustrate this connection, has been the leading theme of these pages, intended both for the student and general reader. The industries and results of their settlements have been so ably treated by Agnew, Smiles, Weiss, and other writers, that repetition on this ground would be superfluous. The thread of history is maintained in various ways; in the actions and correspondence of famous men, combined with an influential policy, I have endeavoured to trace the annals of a people, who nobly sacrificed *all* for conscience' sake.

To gather together new facts, to arrive at fresh evidence, is the duty of every worker in the field of research, and to this end, valuable letters and extracts now appear for the first time.

An eminent scholar has remarked, "There is need of little books on great subjects." If this contribution should form a link in the chain of Protestant history, it will have fulfilled its aim by telling the story of the Refugees "in their English home."

As popular interest is widely recalled by the Two Hundredth Anniversary of the Revocation of the Edict of Nantes, *October*, 1685, so it is trusted that this volume may serve as a fitting tribute to the interesting Commemoration in England and other countries.

My best acknowledgments are due to Messrs. Marcus Ward and Co. for their permission to use the portrait of Coligny, inserted from the life of the Admiral by Walter Besant, M.A., to whom, also, I am kindly indebted.

22nd OCTOBER, 1885.

CONTENTS.

CHAPTER I.

                                                                PAGE

The first settlements—French and Walloons—Learned men in England—Their friendships—Warham, Cranmer, Bucer, Farel, and others—Aid of the English Church and the Universities—Foreign Churches in London—John à Lasco—The Book of Common Prayer in French—Glastonbury—Edward VI. and the reformed religion—Calvin—The Protector Somerset—The Marian persecution and exiles 1

CHAPTER II.

The refugees under Queen Elizabeth—Bishops of London and their aid—Grindal and Parker—Walloons and French at Norwich—Admiral Coligny and his brother Odet—Their character and influence—Opinions of Dr. Bersier—The St. Bartholomew and its results—The Queen's safety

—Canterbury Cathedral and its crypt church—
Archbishops Parker, Grindal, Whitgift, Bancroft,
and Abbot—The reception of the strangers—
Religious controversies—Refugee Church under
James I.   21

CHAPTER III.

Foreign Protestants under Charles I.—Archbishop
Laud and his measures—The Civil War—The
Puritans—Commonwealth—Cromwell—The Restoration—Charles II.—James II.—Revocation
of the "Edict of Nantes"—Its effects in England
and France—Louis XIV.—William III. and his
aid to the refugees—Bishops Compton and Burnet—Archbishops Sancroft and Tillotson—Bishop
Lloyd—Marquis Ruvigny—Queen Anne and her
assistance—Archbishops Tenison, Wake, Herring,
and Secker—Their encouragement of the exiles—
Correspondence with foreign Powers in their behalf—Antoine Court—Close of the persecutions   39

CHAPTER IV.

French churches in London—Their history—Rise and
fall—Threadneedle Street Church—Its ministers
—The Savoy and its foreign services—Historical
memories—Ministers—Somerset House Chapel
—Durham House—The increase of churches in
1685—Spitalfields—Soho—The smaller churches
— Dissension between the "Conformist" and

other communities—Royal Bounty Fund and its history—Distinguished refugees in church annals—Allix—Casaubon—Colomiez—Jortin—Romaine—Famous names in Ireland . . . 74

CHAPTER V.

Suburban congregations—Provincial churches—Rye, Dover, Sandwich, Maidstone, Faversham, Southampton, the Channel Isles—Religious differences—The West of England—East Anglia—Canterbury and the crypt church—Archbishop Tait's encouragement of—Present condition—Historical and refugee names round Canterbury—Its ancient aspect and memories 103

CHAPTER VI.

Refugee documents and archives—Registers of the churches—Somerset House, Record Office, and other libraries—The State Papers—Private and provincial collections — Inscriptions — Archives in Ireland—Printed books—Correspondence—Official and private—The "Savile Letters" and Lord Halifax—Publications of learned societies—Acts of the Synods—Study of the past . . 137

CHAPTER VII.

Present state of French Protestantism—Influence of the English Church abroad—The Coligny Monument — Dr. Bersier and churches in Paris — Foreign societies and their work—America and her co-operation—Churches still remaining—French Protestant Hospital—Archbishop Tait and his influence—Huguenot Society of London—Publications on refugee history—Bi-centenary of the "Revocation of the Edict of Nantes"—Conclusion 151

LIST OF ILLUSTRATIONS.

Entrance to the French Church in Crypt of Canterbury Cathedral . . . . *To face title-page*

Portrait of Admiral Coligny . . . *To face* 31

Medal Commemorative of the Revocation of the Edict of Nantes 73

Page from the Psalms, after Clement Marot . *To face* 145

PROTESTANTS FROM FRANCE IN THEIR ENGLISH HOME.

CHAPTER I.

The first settlements—French and Walloons—Learned men in England—Their friendships—Warham, Cranmer, Bucer, Farel, and others—Aid of the English Church and the Universities—Foreign Churches in London—John à Lasco—The Book of Common Prayer in French—Glastonbury—Edward VI. and the reformed religion—Calvin—The Protector Somerset—The Marian persecution and exiles.

"STRANGERS" is the word often applied to those who, flying to England for religion's sake from the Low Countries and France, have found in our land, a safe asylum from persecution and distress. Their church is frequently alluded to in early writings and documents, and even the simple inscription, "A stranger," on marble tablet, or parish register, records the annals of many an illustrious refugee. The word is now no longer applicable to the exiled bands whose descendants have, in many cases, become one with the tenets of the Church of England. Time, with its relentless power, has bridged over the distinctions which once separated us from those differing on religious grounds. The common struggle for livelihood, for fame or wealth, has united us with the "strangers," in whom we may have found some of our best friends.

The sixteenth century can be said to have caused an awakening in Europe, whether in religion, letters, art, or science. The invention of printing in the previous age—the arrival of learned exiles—their sojourn both in London and at our Universities—all had its influence in forming those events which made England a congenial home for the foreign Protestants. The increase of the Scriptures, their printing at Antwerp and other places abroad, the French and Flemish versions for the Walloon provinces, —such circumstances tended to familiarize and prepare for the reception of those truths which were the precursors of the Reformation. The

Bible began to be read and studied, and some of the leading French reformers advanced its circulation. Of them, Jacques Lefevre, of Etaples, in Picardy, who translated the four Gospels into French in 1523, and his follower, William Farel, stand out in bold relief.

Persecution followed them severely, Farel fled into Switzerland, while the Bibles and Testaments were openly burnt. The truth, however, could not be extinguished, and of this the simple and touching story of "Palissy the potter" affords the greatest proof.

Perhaps few of us associate with the enamelled Palissy ware, the life and trials of that Huguenot artist who, in his greatest distress, made the Bible his consolation. Though his talents brought him into the service of the Catholic nobles, he would not abjure his faith; and it is sad to record, that at the age of seventy-eight, he was arrested and imprisoned in the Bastile, and there died, an example of heroic courage and faith in the Scriptures.

Of almost equal interest is an incident of the preservation of a Bible, which afterwards came into the possession of the family of the Fabers, of literary note.

"This Bible once belonged to M. de Dibon, a Huguenot gentleman who was arrested after the Revocation of the Edict of Nantes (1685); time only was spared to bury the book within a chest in his garden, while Monsieur de Dibon was carried off to prison. He managed to escape, but ere he quitted his native France for ever, determined to revisit his estate to recover his Bible; this he did, and with it in his hand, an impoverished exile, reached England in the reign of William III.!"

The printing of the Scriptures was followed by other works, and the middle of the sixteenth century witnessed many important events as to the increase of religion. For awhile, we must go back to France, to see how the beginning of the Reformation took root there, and how the pioneers of that change found sympathy in England, whither their descendants fled in succeeding periods.

In the snow-crowned mountains of Dauphiny, in the High Alps, at Gap, was born William Farel, one of the famous theologians who was afterwards destined to throw great influence on the reformation abroad, and to be its leader in

France and Switzerland. Even before that time appeared, as we have seen, Lefevre d'Etaples, the patriarch of the reformed doctrine, one of whose first disciples was Farel: in Geneva, where his memory is rightly cherished, he much advanced the growing religion. The arrival of learned foreigners in England and at our Universities was due, in some degree, to the patronage and kindness shown them by our noted divines and statesmen.

Archbishop Warham's prominence in this respect is proverbial, and among his frequent guests at historic Lambeth, was Erasmus, who used to come down by water, from his friend's (Sir Thomas More's) house at Chelsea. Dr. Jortin[1] relates that Erasmus speaks of the Archbishop as a "learned and worthy man, and loves me as though he were my father or brother." The Primate encouraged and helped him when he prepared his Greek Testament and also his Latin translation for press.

It was a saying of Erasmus, "If you would drink deeply of the well-springs of wisdom apply to Greek. Read Plato; he wrote on marble with a diamond; but, above all, read the

[1] "Life of Erasmus," by J. Jortin. 1751-54.

New Testament, 'tis the key to the kingdom of heaven."

Of Erasmus' visits to the Archbishop, he says: "What genius! what erudition! what kindness and modesty! From Warham who ever departed in sorrow?" "But there is a dark side to the highest character, and we cannot but regret that the cruel persecutions which followed the earlier converts to the reformed doctrine were carried on by Warham with a severity which stands in singular contrast to the gentler features of his life." [2]

Erasmus, by his residence in Cambridge, had done much to encourage the revival of learning in England, and this, to an extent, influenced the growth of the Reformation.

In a letter of his to Margaret of Navarre, who had gone to Spain to visit her captive brother, we find Erasmus recommending to her notice John à Lasco, who was afterwards to play so leading a part with the refugees in London.

In Archbishop Cranmer (Warham's successor), history chronicles much relating to our subject. The foundation of the "strangers'" church in

---

[2] "Diocesan History of Canterbury," by the Rev. R. C. Jenkins, M.A., Hon. Canon of Canterbury.

London and Canterbury took place during his primacy. "London was the great centre of intercourse with the Continent, and along with the other wares imported from the Low Countries, there were clandestinely introduced many of the chief writings of the German and Swiss reformers." Many a tradition of old London is rife with the memories of some of the foreign scholars and divines who sought friendly converse with our own. John Colet, Dean of St. Paul's, Roger Ascham, Tremellius, would meet John à Lasco, Peter Martyr, Bucer, and several of like fame.

The two latter had theological appointments, Bucer being at Cambridge, and Peter Martyr at Oxford.

Bucer dedicated some of his works to Archbishop Cranmer, under whose hospitable roof at Lambeth Palace were assembled Fagius, Tremellius, and Peter Alexander (a French refugee from Arles), who resided with the Primate. It was not foreseen how this liberality, on the Archbishop's part, to welcome the strangers, tended to produce those controversies which were inseparable from the spirit of the age.

Bucer, delighted with the novelty and comfort of Cambridge, declared " no college on the continent could compare to our Universities." In his brief professorship, and in the stormy theological contests he there encountered, Bucer's life was short, but eventful, and in his honoured tomb, in St. Mary's church, old animosities seem to have been forgotten, in the respect paid his memory at the last.

A letter, fully corroborating this feeling, was written by Sir John Cheke to Dr. Parker (Dean of Lincoln, afterwards Primate), on the death of Bucer, which spoke of his "deepness of knowledge, his earnestness in religion, his fatherliness in life."

In 1548, Archbishop Cranmer wrote to John à Lasco and Bucer, inviting them to England, and we find Utenhovius, the assistant of John à Lasco, writing from Canterbury to the Primate about this time "that they had sermons and godly meetings within their walls." Their minister was François La Rivière, who afterwards held a similar position at the French and Walloon Church in London.

This would seem to indicate some sort of congregation at Canterbury, and in another two years, 1550, we can speak of its foundation and of the countenance afforded it by Royalty, and subsequently of the patronage gracefully extended to it, by many among our Archbishops.

It must not be supposed that although Cranmer corresponded with, and encouraged Protestants to England, he was free from doctrines with which many of them greatly differed. The phases of theological controversy only come within the limits of this subject, as an incidental illustration of refugee history, and their full scope must be sought in larger works.

It may be stated that what is known as "Cranmer's Catechism," in which the Primate's orthodoxy on the sacraments was doubted, was the point of attack by many foreign divines, and that in reply to the allegations therein, the Archbishop consulted John à Lasco and Peter Martyr.

The year 1550, however, dates the establishment of a congregation in London, presided over by John à Lasco, and the charter of Edward VI. granting St. Austin's Church, the disused convent of the Augustinian Friars, to the strangers, on 24th of July in that year.

We have now arrived at defined ground in the annals of this subject, and shall be able to sketch its progress, and a corresponding activity in churches afterwards established in the provinces.

Stow, in his "Survey of London," after describing St. Anthony's Hospital in Threadneedle Street, which was dissolved at the Reformation, and its revenues annexed to St. George's Chapel, Windsor, says, "The houses with others be letten out for rent, and the church is a preaching-place for the French nation."

A "superintendent," John à Lasco, and four "ministers," were appointed by letters patent to have the general oversight of the foreign churches. We learn Bishop Ridley was opposed to the scheme, but that Cranmer favoured it. The noted work, by John à Lasco, was now translated into French, "Toute la forme et maniere du ministere ecclesiastique en l'Eglise des estrangers à Londres, 1556," and adopted as the standard code for the foreign congregations. Their services became a duly recognized institution; but it is difficult, at this early date, to identify the ministers of their first church.

In the pages of the diarists and writers of the time, references are made to some congregations, and in Henry Mackyn's diary (Mackyn being a London citizen) occurs the following :—

24 June, 1557.—" Goodly service kept at the Frère Austens by the merchandes strangers as has bene sent."

In 1559 we read, " The 7 day of Octobre dyd pryche within the [Queen's] Chapell at Whyt-hall, parson Veron the French-[man]."

Richard Vauville, sometimes called Richard François, succeeded La Rivière in the Walloon church, and Beza's testimony of the former is not without comment : " Il est mort, ministre de l'eglise Françoise de Frankfort après la dissipation de celle en Angleterre où il avait long tems servi très heureusement."

The allusion to Frankfort was on the flight of the exiles in Queen Mary's reign, many of whom escaped to that city. Pierre Alexandre, in 1561, was befriended by Cranmer, and was one of the early ministers of their church ; to him succeeded, Jean Cousin. Nicholas de Saules, another pastor, is said to have attended, at Admiral Coligny's request, the famous " Colloquy " at Poissy, made memorable in the after struggles of Protestantism, and the precursor of the " St. Bartholomew."

The fuller account of this church and its ministers will be found in Chapter IV.

As a landmark of refugee history, the printing of the Common Prayer in French,[3] for which a patent was granted in 1552, forms a most decided advance. Sir William Cecil, Dr. Goodrich (Bishop of Ely), and the Lord Chancellor, equally with the Protector Somerset, advocated and supported this movement with Edward VI.

The translation was made by one Françoys Philippe, and the success of the undertaking was due to John à Lasco and Archbishop Cranmer, and is memorable in every way.

Permission was given for a French Protestant to set up a press, and Thomas Gaultier, the printer of the Prayer-book, had that privilege.

The early history, both of the Dutch church in Austin Friars and that of the French and Walloon Church in Threadneedle Street, is in these times, much intermixed and difficult to trace in due sequence. We read that in 1552, owing to

---

[3] "Le Livre des Prières communes, de l'administration des Sacramens et autres cérémonies en l'Église d'Angleterre. 1553."

some of John à Lasco's congregation not resorting to their parish churches, they were threatened with imprisonment, and that à Lasco appealed to the king, that they might have a royal warrant not to be disturbed in the exercise of their worship.

One of the eminent men at this time was Rudolf Cavalier, who assisted Tremellius in teaching Hebrew at Cambridge. For his gratuitous lectures in that University, he was made a free denizen, and afterwards a Prebend of Canterbury Cathedral.

We now hear of the refugee settlement at Glastonbury, of itself an important and memorable event, revealing as it did, the great care that the Protector Somerset took to support the cause of the exiles, by planting the weaving trade in that town, where he had acquired estates. Sir William Cecil and Cranmer were also interested in the establishment of this church, and by their means one Pollanus was appointed "superintendent." The death of the Duke of Somerset very much disturbed the work of the exiles; their employment was well-nigh gone, and in their distress they applied to the government for assistance.

That being granted, their occupations were resumed, and in this matter, Pollanus had taken great trouble. On the decease, however, of Edward VI. the congregation was dispersed, and many fled to Frankfort.

The settlement had consisted both of Walloons and French, and their liturgy was framed on the lines of that at Strasbourg, where Valerand Poulain, or Pollandus, had been pastor before coming to Glastonbury. The foundation of this church appears to show clearly the relations of our policy with foreign communities, and perhaps more than all, a certain sympathy between Cranmer and the Protector Somerset on religious matters. Their service contained passages which are to this day used by the French Protestants, so that in many respects, a unique and historical interest gathers round this " strangers' " church.

We now turn, for a time, from England to the Continent, as it is impossible not to include the efforts of the Reformers abroad, some of whom much influenced the work which was progressing at home.

Calvin, born at Noyon in 1509, claims our notice, while Beza adds to the group of learned divines. The last-named took a prominent part in the famous colloquy at Poissy in 1561, between the Roman Catholic church and the Huguenots, of whom he was the representative spokesman.

Calvin's influence was, perhaps of all the rest, most felt in England, and the controversies which occurred with other leading men at Strasbourg and Frankfort caused, though in an incipient way, the first appearance of English Puritanism. The long disputations between Calvin and his opponents do not come within the limits of this work, and can be studied in the pages of Hardwick's "Church History," and other standard books. It may be said that on Beza the mantle of Calvin descended, and that he was very much associated with the struggles of the Huguenots in France, and with the action of the English bishops.

Of Calvin's intercourse and correspondence with England, most interesting letters[4] remain, which have been printed from the MSS. preserved in the archives at Geneva.

With Edward VI. and Archbishop Cranmer, Calvin kept up much communication, and the

[4] "Letters of John Calvin," edited by Dr. Jules Bonnet; 2 vols. 1855.

direct tenour of his views that the closer union of the reformed churches would be effected by the assembling of general synods, was fully shared in by the Primate. Calvin writes to Cranmer that "nothing is more powerful to unite the churches of God than the pure teaching of the Gospel, and harmony of faith. For this cause I desire that pious and learned men should meet together on the principal points of doctrine."

Calvin proposed to the Protector Somerset, in 1548, a plan for the complete reformation of the English Church, and although much difference was expressed at his doctrines, yet their influence was wide and important. The French Church in London had, in its early days, been troubled with theological disputes, and Calvin's intervention was sought.

Geneva, where the reformer long lived, retains grateful memories of his benefactions. In truth, he laid the foundation of much of her theological fame, or, as ably described by the late J. R. Green, the historian, "that his influence made Geneva from 1541 the centre of the Protestant world."

On the death of Edward, Calvin wrote a

letter of great regret, and in the lifetime of that monarch much correspondence passed between the throne of England and the reformer.

To Calvin, the King addressed these memorable words:—" It is a great thing to be a king, and especially of such a country; and yet I doubt not, that you regard it as above all comparison greater, to be a Christian."

The reign of Edward, though short, was naturally much in unison with Protestant sympathies, which had been aroused by Roger Ascham, Dr. Coxe, and others, who had early taught the reformed doctrines and truth to their Royal master.

In 1553, Calvin and Cranmer used their influence with the French king, to liberate one of his subjects imprisoned for the Gospel's sake.

As time progressed, the central figure, however, was Archbishop Cranmer, who, as we have seen, invited foreigners to London for a general conference on the union of Protestant Churches. To Edward, at the beginning of his reign, the "strangers" appealed upon this projected scheme, which was not greatly encouraged.

The loss of the king, and previously that of the

Protector Somerset, extinguished all hopes of any further progress in the refugee cause, and the accession of Queen Mary witnessed a complete overthrow of the previous efforts to strengthen or consolidate the foreign Protestant faith in England.

John à Lasco had leave to embark for the Low Countries, and finally settled at Frankfort, where a congregation had been founded. It is touching to record that when Cranmer was ordered by Queen Mary to keep his house at Lambeth (which, alas! he soon exchanged for the Tower), many of those whom he had befriended came and consoled him, and among them Peter Martyr, his former guest.

A royal inquisition ordered the foreigners who had settled in London to leave England. "That city," says the late J. R. Green, "retained much of its Protestant sympathy, but over the rest of the country the tide of reaction swept without a check." "Each step in the Queen's persecution had been marked by a fresh flight of preachers, merchants, and gentry across the seas."

Among the exiles we find some who became bishops and statesmen in the succeeding reign.

Sir Francis Knollys was at Frankfort, and Bishops Horne, Parkhurst, Aylmer, Jewel, and Cox sought refuge in distant lands.

Even a Roman Catholic writer gave his thoughts on the atrocities of the Marian persecution.

"At times, indeed, a momentary suspension of cruelty seemed to indicate the presence of a milder spirit. But the illusion was quickly dissipated, new commissions were issued, new barbarities were enacted, and a monument of infamy was erected, which even at the distance of three centuries cannot be regarded without horror."[5]

From the flight and persecution of the refugees, in these direful times, it is well to remember that the Reformation had *begun*, and was only undergoing that transient decay from which it was to emerge in brighter power, and to show enduring results, sadly purchased, however, by the sacrifice of those whose sufferings have ennobled the history of all time.

"In that strange century," says Dr. Bersier, "in which exalted mysticism was often found

---

[5] Dodd, "Church History of England," vol. ii.

allied with the usual degradation of the paganism of the Renaissance, this beautiful plant of the Reformation grew up, producing as its flowers the Protestant family home, and men and women of so grand and true a type that they make the name of Huguenot for ever fragrant in the field of history." [6]

[6] "Earlier Life of Coligny," by Eugène Bersier, D.D.

CHAPTER II.

The refugees under Queen Elizabeth—Bishops of London and their aid—Grindal and Parker—Walloons and French at Norwich—Admiral Coligny and his brother Odet—Their character and influence—Opinions of Dr. Bersier—The St. Bartholomew and its results—The Queen's safety—Canterbury Cathedral and its crypt church—Archbishops Parker, Grindal, Whitgift, Bancroft, and Abbot—Their reception of the strangers—Religious controversies—Refugee church under James I.

A VERY important page of refugee history now opens before us.

The reign of Elizabeth comprises some of the most eventful stages of progress, though reached through much warfare and controversy. During this period occurred the St. Bartholomew and its consequences on the foreign settlements in England—the life and death of the hero of that massacre, Admiral Coligny, and the strengthening of the Reformation in England by the influences of the Huguenot faith in our land.

"The trading-classes of the town," says Green, in his "History of the English people," "had been the first to embrace the doctrines of the Reformation; but their Protestantism became a passion as the refugees of the continent brought to shop and market their tale of outrage and blood."

The features with which we are mostly concerned, reveal the encouragement given to the refugee worship and their churches, through the instrumentality of the Primates Parker, Grindal, Whitgift, and the Bishops of London. The foreign policy of Elizabeth is clearly shown by the aid she afforded to French Protestants in their internal wars, receiving, in return, that help in her kingdom by which it was partly secured from the factions of the Romanists.

"The Reformation was fighting for Elizabeth on the one side of the sea as the other."

Her reign witnessed the reunion of the Huguenot church in London, which, under the rule of Queen Mary, had been dispersed, and almost annihilated.

At the end of the sixteenth century we hear

of more congregations, while those already existing, especially at Norwich and Canterbury, were encouraged and increased.

It is well known that Elizabeth proceeded with great caution in her gradual development of the Protestant religion, and that the historical site of Paul's Cross often witnessed her presence to hear the discourses of noted men. In 1559, a year after her accession, Strype's "Annals of the Reformation" record, that "Mr. Veron, a Frenchman by birth, a learned Protestant and pastor of St. Martin's, Ludgate, preached at Paul's Cross before the Mayor and aldermen. After the sermon they sang, all in common, a psalm in metre, the custom being brought from abroad by the exiles."

Matthew Parker, Archbishop of Canterbury, and Edmund Grindal, Bishop of London, are two pioneers of refugee history for the next twenty years.

In Parker, the valued chaplain to her mother, Queen Ann Boleyn, Elizabeth "found an agent in the re-organization of the church, whose patience and moderation were akin to her own."[1]

In the beginning of the Primate's career, great

[1] Green's "History of the English People."

difficulties beset his work. Dean Hook, in his
" Lives of the Archbishops," remarks that " Protestantism was degenerating into Puritanism, and he perceived that even the men with whom he would have to act could not be depended upon."

Many exiles had returned from abroad, influenced by their foreign sojourn, and it was the wise policy of the Archbishop, jointly with Cecil (Lord Burleigh), to conciliate them. A certain catholicity of thought pervaded the Primate, as we perceive, in a letter from him to that statesman, regarding the conference at Poissy between Roman Catholics and Protestants.

" If we all were as careful to help the re-edifying of so great a Church as France is to Christ again, beside the commodity which should redound to that realm, it could not but turn to our quiet at home, to have more friends in conjunction of religion."[2]

Our interest seems often diverted from Grindal, as Bishop of London, to Archbishop Parker, between whom genial friendship had long existed. Both of these men had much to do with the refugees, and a recommendation

[2] (Parker Society) " Correspondence of Matthew Parker." 1853.

from Bishop Grindal to the Primate on their behalf, generally led to a successful issue.

After the departure of John à Lasco, Queen Elizabeth chose Grindal as "superintendent" of the foreign churches. His care for them is recorded by Strype, who relates: "He did show himself on all occasions a true patron to them." The Queen, with searching keenness, required the French and Dutch ministers in 1562 to give Grindal a list of their communicants.

In 1567 the Bishop issued an inquiry throughout every ward in London, of their trades, occupations, &c., and to what churches they resorted. This proceeding was of twofold value—in gaining a better estimate of the number of refugees, and also of protection for them when threatened with persecution. In 1568 we find the minister and elders of the French church gave in the names of all their members, as the Dutch community had previously done: the ministers were Jean Cousin, Pierre Chastellain, Anthony de Pouchel; the elders, Michael Chaudron and Gerard de Lobel. These returns were sent in to the Bishop of London, and afterwards to the Primate, from whom redress or aid could be obtained.

Grindal's opinion of Jean Cousin is seen in his letter[3] to Beza in 1568, as follows: "Master John Cousin, the most faithful minister of the French church in this country, has this day shown me a letter that he has written to you on the state of the Dutch church in London." The subject alluded to was the controversial war then raging on doctrinal questions.

Jean Cousin also interposed with Lord Burleigh, and obtained the liberation of all the refugees detained in prison for debt; his correspondence was often associated with letters from the Queen and Beza.

The dissensions above referred to in the foreign churches occasioned Grindal much trouble; he severely dealt with disunion, obliging the renunciation of erroneous opinion. We have thus seen, how the wise policy of Elizabeth, followed by Bishop Grindal, was carried out by Archbishop Parker. Not only the congregation in London came under his cognizance, but the provincial churches sought his valued recognition.

Thus, as regards the Walloons at Norwich,

[3] Letters, Parker Society: Bishop Grindal.

communications followed between the Duke of Norfolk and the Primate in 1565.

"Since my coming home the strangers hath been suitors to me, for my letters to you for the having of a church, whereupon I talked with the Bishop (Parkhurst)[1] and others of the city, by whom I hear as well of their good order in religion as also of their honest conversation; here, the churches that I know be void, that upon your letters to the Bishop and the Mayor they will take present order."[1]

Archbishop Parker, a native of Norwich, might have had some partiality for the traditions of that ancient city, but it does not appear that he was influenced other than by just motives in all matters affecting the refugees.

The settlement there had been increased by many from Sandwich, in Kent; and in 1563 we have a letter of the Primate to Sir W. Cecil, saying, "The strangers being very godly on the Sabbath-day, and busy in their work on the week-day, their quietness such as the Mayor and his brethren have no cause of variance coming before them."

Unfortunately this union did not always exist,

[1] Parker Society.

for in 1571 Bishop Parkhurst (Norwich) writes to Bullinger about the dissensions: "You will scarce believe what labour I have undergone, to say nothing of expense during the whole time, and yet these refractory people will not give up a single point. The congregation was near being broken up. In the French Church everything is very quiet; they are in number about 400."[5]

It will be remembered that the Walloon church was jointly used by the French refugees, who were much increased in numbers after the St. Bartholomew (1572).

With so just an advocate of religious freedom as the Archbishop, and the sympathy of Bishop Grindal, it is not to be wondered that England should receive a large portion of those who escaped the St. Bartholomew massacre.

The event is so well known in history that to dilate upon it would be apart from my object, further than to expatiate on the enormity of that cruel act which desolated thousands of homes, and upon the death of the leader of the Huguenots, Admiral Coligny, whose courage and constant faith are now being better appreciated through the narrative of his life, by the

[5] Zurich Letters, Parker Society.

Rev. Pasteur Bersier, D.D.,[6] of Paris ; and also by the graphic pen of Walter Besant, M.A., in his monograph of that patriot-statesman.

We are concerned rather on the *influence* of the St. Bartholomew *in our own land*, wherein its consequences were no less momentous than true. For the exodus from France brought many nobles, the learned, the wealthy, the poor, and the suffering to our shores. A few years before, Odet de Coligny (Cardinal Châtillon), the brother of the Admiral, was ambassador in England. On his arrival in November, 1567, he was met by Sir Thomas Gresham, who conducted him to his house in London, and the morning after, a very interesting circumstance is recorded by the historian Camden. "The Cardinal, in his short cloak and rapier by his side, rode with Sir Thomas Gresham and other persons of distinction to the French church, to show his approbation of the Protestant religion."

Sir Thomas Gresham will be remembered as the founder of the first Royal Exchange, opened by Queen Elizabeth in 1570, and destroyed in the Great Fire of 1666. In that cloistered

---

[6] "Earlier Life of Admiral Coligny," by Eugène Bersier. London, 1884.

quadrangle would be merchants of every nation, known by their distinctive dress and language, forming indeed, a picturesque scene of "Old London." We soon after read of Odet Coligny being presented at court, "where he had an audience of the Queen, and was graciously received, which induced him to remain in England as long as he lived."

It is sad to record that his death was alleged to be that of poison at Canterbury in 1570; and among the historic monuments in the east end of that noble Minster, a small and unpretending vaulted tomb marks the resting-place of the brother of the illustrious Admiral.

It would be unfair to the cause of Coligny to leave unnoticed the remark of Dr. Bersier, "that the language of Queen Elizabeth (in a letter she addressed to her ambassador in Paris) seems to us to describe with singular exactness the very part Coligny was playing at this moment; truly devoted to the Protestant cause, he was resolved to uphold it only by lawful means."

The letter was as follows:—" Greet the Admiral affectionately in our name, and assure him that the wisdom and constancy which he has displayed hitherto and his whole behaviour

COLIGNY.

To face page 31.

have deserved and have won for him the admiration of the world. Let him not now, therefore, neglect the cause of God, of which his conscience assures him he is so good a witness, but let him use his wisdom in the furtherance of that cause." (Elizabeth's despatches to Throckmorton, March 31, 1562.)

As time progresses, the central figure of that great and sanguinary drama comes out more and more clearly, as we view him with the one aim of upholding that truth from which he never swerved, amid the incessant religious conflicts which characterized the sixteenth century. Even Bossuet said, "All the attempts made to decry the Admiral had only rendered his memory more illustrious."[7] His biographer, Dr. Bersier, also remarks, "Coligny presented the noble example of a pure and beautiful home-life, in which austerity of purpose was blended with the utmost tenderness of heart, an example rare indeed in that dissolute age."

To his old castle home of Châtillon-sur-Loing, in the precincts of which he sleeps his "last sleep," many a traveller might well bend

---

[7] Macaulay speaks of him as "the good Coligny."

his steps and revive some recollections of this hero-martyr of 1572.

The influence of the St. Bartholomew on the seats of learning in England cannot be unnoticed. In his history of the University of Cambridge, the Rev. J. B. Mullinger remarks, "The exultation of Sander and Louvain only brought into stronger relief the honest indignation of Parker and Cambridge." The French envoy had to listen while Elizabeth, forgetful of her wonted guile, and rising to the full height of her imperial nature, uttered words of true womanly scorn—while Burleigh, as he too laid aside his habitual wariness, declared in the council chamber that no more atrocious crime had disgraced humanity since the crucifixion of the Founder of their common faith." The effect of this event on Cambridge was to strengthen the spirit of Protestantism, which that University had, to a certain extent, imbibed. The massacre was the theme and cause of many a political letter, or record of chronicler, whether ecclesiastic or lay. The Pope's denunciation of the arrival of the refugees after 1572 was answered by Bishop Jewel

(Salisbury), who thus wrote, "Is it not lawful for the Queen to receive strangers without the Pope's warrant? They are good examples of virtue, faith, and patience, the towns in which they abide are happy, for God doth follow them with his blessings." This remark has been endorsed almost to a word, in later times by Southey, who said, "Wherever the refugees from the French persecution fled, a blessing attended them." On October 27th, 1572, Archbishop Parker, at the Queen's command, put forth special prayers for the persecuted and persecutors, a copy of which is printed in "Strype's" life of that Primate. The prelates were loyal for Elizabeth, fearing for her life, and one of them wrote to Lord Burleigh that "the Bishops feared not the mangling of their bodies, but we dread the hurt of our Head, meaning the Queen, for therein consisteth our life and safety." The times were very critical, the mass was still celebrated in many churches, and Dr. Parker had secret court enemies.

The exodus from France naturally increased the various congregations, and to a great extent, that, in the crypt church of Canterbury Cathedral. In 1573 the Primate recommends its wants to the Dean and Chapter; and we find him, in a letter to Lord Burleigh, stating "For those ministers of France exiled, I did not only procure by collection a good portion, but also gave them of my own purse a large and honest portion among them, which I have not yet much blazed, nor intend not; let other men delight in their 'Gloria Patri,' I will do but what I can, quietly."[8]

In the splendid banquets to his Sovereign at Canterbury, it may be that the words spoken by Archbishop Parker on another occasion, "That profitable and gentle strangers ought to be welcomed and not to be grudged at," would re-echo in his mind, as he conducted the Queen over that historic minster, the crypt of which she had granted to the use of the foreigners, whose industries were already benefiting the metropolitical City.

In 1575 the scene changes — Archbishop Grindal, in succeeding to the primacy, continued the aid to the refugees which he had shown them as Bishop of London. His short tenure of the See, from 1575—1583, did not enable him to exercise the liberality of his pre-

[8] Parker Society.

decessor, and his falling under the censure of Elizabeth, and his premature resignation, crippled his otherwise wide influence.

In Archbishop Whitgift, we had a prelate differing in many points from Parker and Grindal, and it is the more to be recorded that he supported the cause of the exiles, and that the Queen acted on his advice, and regarded him as a personal friend. In 1591, John Castoll, a "discreet and learned man," was minister of the French church in London, and by his intercession with the Archbishop, arranged a somewhat difficult matter in favour of his congregation, who were expected by the Queen to contribute in money towards the assistance of Henry of Navarre, who was trying for the crown of France.

Castoll's statements that his congregation could not assist, having to send what funds they had to the relief of the churches at Montpellier, Geneva, and places abroad, were supported by the Primate and Lord Burleigh.

We afterwards find Mr. Castoll corresponding with the Archbishop, who in those days often advised on foreign as well as on ecclesiastical and civil matters. Encouragement was given at this time to many trades, and the erection of a wool staple was an industry in which the different refugee communities participated.

With James I. the fugitives enjoyed the same liberty as under Queen Elizabeth, though we do not read of such direct assistance given them. The King said, " I will protect you as it becomes a good prince to protect all who have abandoned their country for religion's sake." (*Archives, French Church, London.*)

James's character was peaceable, though leisurely, and inclined to take matters smoothly, he wrote to the French ambassador: " If the Queen, your mistress, chooses to infringe the edicts granted to the Protestants of her kingdom, I do not admit that the alliance I have made and confirmed with France shall prevent my aiding and protecting them."

Richard Bancroft was Archbishop of Canterbury during part of James I.'s reign, and there are occasional instances when his assistance was valuable and important.

The new translation of the Scriptures was now undertaken, and what is known as the authorized version—following the conference of learned men at Hampton Court—was published in 1611. The condition, or rather legislative action, as to the churches in the Channel Isles, came under the Primate's notice; the congregations there, having overstepped their bounds, their authority had to be curtailed. The differences between the Church of England and the French Protestants were long, and although Dr. Bancroft began the work of adjustment, his successor (Abbot) completed the task.

We find several instances of that Primate's regard for the "strangers."

There had been, about the year 1620, a considerable migration from France, and we read that the Archbishop "commends the cause of the distressed French to the tender affection of the bishops and clergy, and urges them to interest others in their behalf, according to a request which had gone out from the council of the nation."

There were also some negotiations for the improvement of foreign trade and the prohibition of the importation of silk goods; such matters were usually addressed to the King, but in many cases were first considered by the Archbishop or the Lord Chancellor.

As the spiritual power in the realm became

more and more distinct from the secular, the relations of the English Church, as associated with the foreign, draw closer and closer.

One could not have wished it otherwise, though in many cases the independent action of the latter was too much fettered by episcopacy.

The last years of Abbot's primacy merge into the reign of Charles I., and in the eventful course of that period, when the absolutism of Archbishop Laud was so prominent, we shall see how his influence reduced to a level of inaction the earnestness of those refugee churches which, through trial and patience, had risen to much excellence.

CHAPTER III.

Foreign Protestants under Charles I.—Archbishop Laud and his measures—The Civil War—The Puritans—Commonwealth — Cromwell — The Restoration—Charles II.—James II.—Revocation of the "Edict of Nantes"—Its effects in England and France—Louis XIV.—William III. and his aid to the refugees—Bishops Compton and Burnet—Archbishops Sancroft and Tillotson—Bishop Lloyd—Marquis Ruvigny—Queen Anne and her assistance—Archbishops Tenison, Wake, Herring, and Secker—Their encouragement of the exiles—Correspondence with foreign powers in their behalf—Antoine Court—Close of the persecutions.

WHEN we enter on the reign of Charles I. a different prospect dawns on us. The court influence was not favourable to the refugee element in England. Laud, though Bishop of London, was practically at the head of ecclesiastical affairs. The King, at the beginning of his reign, showed a certain liberality towards the "strangers," and in 1626 issued a decree enjoining all officers of the crown to maintain the numbers of the foreign churches. The Bishops, however, as we shall see later on, opposed this movement, fearing that it would diminish the reputation and dignity of the Episcopal government.

The results of this measure are set forth in the pages of the late J. R. Green's "History of the English People." "The freedom of worship which had been allowed to the Huguenot refugees from France, or the Walloons from Flanders, was suddenly withdrawn, and the requirement of conformity with the Anglican ritual drove them in crowds from the southern ports to seek toleration in Holland. The English ambassador at Paris was forbidden to visit the Huguenot conventicle at Charenton."

Charles was brought much into contact with foreign powers, and it is to be regretted that his complicity with Archbishop Laud, should have diverted his proceedings into a marked insincerity of action.

If the King had pursued a tolerant course towards the Protestants, history would not have recorded the disaster of La Rochelle with so much bitterness against the Sovereign of England.

The Huguenots furnished stores for the English for this expedition, and the conduct of Charles in betraying the inhabitants to the vengeance of the French king, cannot be exonerated.

The result of this affair was, that many of the privileges of the Protestants were taken from them, though Richelieu interceded with Louis XIII. for greater leniency.

In turning from political to ecclesiastical events, which more concern this subject, we find the same policy pursued. The strict injunctions of Archbishop Laud that the foreign congregations should resort to their parish churches, produced discord and ill-will, and many of the ministers, rather than submit to these restraints, left the kingdom. Indeed, the Primate went so far as to designate the Dutch churches at Sandwich and Maidstone "nurseries of unconformity."

It is a question of history how the Archbishop's influence in introducing the English liturgy into Scotland was a fatal mistake, and that it was one of the steps which led to the Civil War, to his own overthrow, and that of his Royal master.

It is not then to be wondered at that the Protestant party of France should take umbrage at the innovations made in regard to their refugee brethren in this country. Both King and Primate acted in concert, and if the former had sincerely held the essentials of Protestantism, no complaints could have been made by the Huguenots, whose progress was constantly checked by Archbishop Laud. Charles, we may say, did show consideration to other than the French refugees, as we learn that in 1634 a collection for the distressed ministers of the Palatinate was set on foot by the King, but discountenanced by the Archbishop. We find the same action in Norwich diocese, where, in Bishop Wren's visitation in 1636, several injunctions were issued for a stricter discipline of the foreign churches; the order for conformity of worship having been so strict that Dr. Jessop, in his "Diocesan History of Norwich," states that the "exodus from that city to New England this year is said by the historian of America to have exceeded 2000." One would have imagined that motives of policy would have actuated the Bishop in retaining an industrious portion of the community, many of whom, on the passing of this severe sentence, left, to the "lessening of manufactures, and transporting their mystery into foreign parts." This emigration, though at a loss to England, through the severity of episcopal jurisdiction, gained to America many an historical and commercial advantage. The tolerance there allowed, spoke in strong contrast to that in the old country, and America has always shown herself a generous advocate of religious freedom.

The episcopate of John Jegon (Norwich) is a contrast to his successor, Matthew Wren.

In 1603 the French congregation petitioned Bishop Jegon against "alien strangers for not contributing to the expense of the church."

This action would indicate that this community looked upon the Bishop as an adviser and arbitrator, and not as a stern assertor of absolutism, at whatever cost to others.

The Commonwealth greatly changed the course of ecclesiastical affairs, and also the relations with the refugee churches.

Cromwell, like Elizabeth, judiciously used the foreign influence to the strengthening of England, and as regards the persecution of the Vaudois by Louis XIV., he made that monarch's minister ashamed of the part he had allowed the French troops to play. The Protector's influence with the Duke of Savoy was such that the edict against the Vaudois was revoked. It is well known that Cromwell's envoy, Sir Samuel Morland, was sent to their relief, also with pecuniary aid, and that the important correspondence of this expedition is preserved among the Cambridge University MSS.

The intercourse at this time between the Universities of Saumur, Sedan, Nismes, &c., and the theological centres of our land was extensive; many French Protestants were incorporated into the University of Oxford, and all of them reached fame and distinction.

The disintegration of church property during the Commonwealth led to various changes, and in its redistribution, several poor livings were augmented.

Cromwell had granted the chapel in Somerset House for the use of the refugees, and, in other ways, by encouragement and relief, showed his sympathy with the "strangers."

In 1653 we hear of a petition of the wardens

of the several handicraft guilds in London that the requests of the French and Walloon churches might be heard, and in 1656 a petition of John Durant, preacher in Canterbury Cathedral, that the societies for maintenance of ministers settle on him 75*l*. per annum.

The result of the Commonwealth rule in church matters is described by the historian J. R. Green, that it " solved, so far as practical working was concerned, the problem of a religious union among Protestants on the base of a wide variety of Christian opinion." " From the church which was thus reorganized, all power of interference with creeds differing from its own was resolutely withheld. Cromwell remained true throughout to his great cause of religious liberty." This would naturally awaken kindly sentiments, and the same feeling seems to have been entertained for his son, Richard Cromwell, for in 1650, the foreign churches congratulated him as Protector, to which he returned a gracious answer.

With the Restoration, another page of history opens before us—a page that is very interesting to study, a period from 1660—1685, the twenty-five years preceding the Revocation of the

Edict of Nantes, and the reigns of Charles II. and James II.

In those years, the varying tendencies of the two monarchs are clearly seen in their conduct towards the foreign Protestants. Though, at times, much countenance was given to them, the underlying influence of Roman Catholicism was at work, fomented by the friendship and influence of Louis XIV. This period also witnessed the advent on the scene of some noted divines, whose part was more effectually played out after the Revocation of the Edict. I allude to Bishops Compton (London) and Burnet (Salisbury), able and zealous supporters of the reformed religion of France, as exercised by the exiles in England.

The opening career of Charles II. sounded fair and firm to the Protestant cause. "Rest assured," said he, "that under our protection you shall have as much liberty as ever you had under my predecessors."

The Gallican ministers assured those in England that the King is a very good Protestant, and much in their behalf. A few years wrought a change in this country, a change which affected all religious creeds.

There are instances of the refugees seeking that consideration which had been given them in former reigns; for in 1660 we read of a petition of the ministers, elders, &c., of the congregation in London for compensation of privileges, that no other French church may be permitted to divide and ruin them.

Charles granted them a place of worship in the Savoy, of which Pepys, the diarist, records a visit on September 24th, 1662: "To the French church in the Savoy, where they have the Common Prayer-book read in French; and which I never saw before, the minister do preach with his hat off, I suppose in further conformity with our church."

This, the first French version of the English liturgy, was by John Durel, and licensed to be used in 1663, as appears by the approval of Bishop Sheldon of London.

We then find an order for this translation to be used as soon as printed in all the parish churches of Jersey and Guernsey, and the King recommending Monsieur Durel for the sinecure now held by the Bishop of Galloway. On February 2nd, 1679, Evelyn records that "Dr. Durel, Dean of Windsor, preached at Whitehall, and read the whole sermon out of his notes, which I had never before seen a Frenchman do, he being of Jersey, and bred at Paris." The wearisome differences between the Walloons and French were always arising, and in 1662 among the "Domestic Papers" in the Record Office, occurs an order "enjoining the Walloons to unite in their worship, to avoid disputes—maintain their own poor—without burdening the city, not to be taxed to maintain other than their own poor."

Certainly, in Charles' reign, no great hindrances were thrown into holding services, though the aid afforded had not been so much as formerly.

An instance of a certain liberality in action can be recorded as to the refugee congregation at Thorney, in Cambridgeshire, who were allowed to choose their own minister, with the approval of the Duke of Bedford and the Bishop of Ely.

The Act of Uniformity passed in 1662 (on St. Bartholomew's Day) was sweeping and entire in its results, and convulsed the ecclesiastical system. "By its rejection of all but episcopal orders, this act severed the Church of England irretrievably from the general body of the Protestant Churches, whether Lutheran or reformed. It was the close of an effort which had been going on ever since Elizabeth's accession, to bring the English communion into closer relations with the reformed communions of the Continent, and into greater harmony with the religious instincts of the nation at large."[1]

The results of this measure are too well known to enlarge on here; the ejected ministers suffered poverty and great distress, and often ended their days in prison.

The King seems to have promoted the interests of some of the foreign pastors. We learn in 1666, he resolves to grant to one Louis Herault the next vacant prebend in Windsor or Westminster. Herault was descended from a family in Normandy, who had become distinguished at Canterbury.

The political privileges of the refugees were not overlooked, for Charles in 1681, ordered that French Protestants should receive, free of expense, letters patent of denization under the Great Seal.

An interest was now taken in those fugitives, who, warned by the approaching advent of the

[1] "History of the English People," by J. R. Green.

Revocation of the Edict of Nantes, escaped to England a few years before that event. We learn in 1683 that a subscription was raised for the relief of the exiled ministers, and that it was supported by Bishop Barlow of Lincoln, and that the Archdeacons in that diocese were asked to join the movement.

Though Charles may not have greatly helped the cause of the strangers, he did not discourage their efforts, a fact the more to be recorded, as history avows his leaning to Catholicism, and that in his last moments, a Romish priest was summoned to his bedside.

Good Bishop Ken and Archbishop Sancroft were also there with messages of mercy, when the latter's well-known and honest speech, historical now in its force, was spoken: "It is time to speak out, sir, for you are about to appear before a Judge who is no respecter of persons."

James II. had been king hardly a year when in October, 1685, was signed the "Revocation of the Edict of Nantes," one of the most memorable and important events to France and our own country.

England was in a great measure prepared to

receive these persecuted and faithful adherents for their religion, as we have seen some of them had arrived beforehand, and the policy of the King, though attracted to Rome, was in favour of continuing the ancient immunities of the foreign Protestants.

We regret to say that James chiefly sought his advisers from the Romish party; and that, though assuming a favourable guise at first, revenged himself on a Bishop of London whom he excluded from his councils, for sympathy with the "strangers." Another instance of the King's intolerance on this matter was that he sided against Monsieur Claude's book on the persecutions in France, the work having been brought to the Royal Exchange and there burnt.

Lord Macaulay also records "that James gave orders that none should receive a crust of bread or basket of coals who did not first take the sacrament according to the Anglican ritual."[2] We cannot ignore the fact that the "briefs," or collections, which were made in this king's reign were open to suspicion, and that the moneys so collected were designed for French papists, or

[2] "History of England," vol. ii.

that it was a political movement with James to make way with the Protestants.

It is impossible not to notice the action and effects of the Revocation of the Edict in France, ere it wrought those changes in England which led to a greater union of the Protestants of the two countries. Every hindrance was put on leaving, so that the very rigour of the Act compelled them to fly from their native land.

It is astonishing to find that some of the estimable people approved of these persecutions. Even Madame de Sévigné, noted for her good sense, writes to the Comte de Bussy :—

"You have doubtless seen the edict by which the king revokes that of Nantes. Nothing can be more admirable than its contents, and no king has done, or ever will do, a more honourable act." The result, however, signally failed in many respects, for, instead of crushing the religion of these persecuted people, it provoked many, accustomed only to their native *patois*, to preach in excellent French. From the cruelties of 1685, arose the great movement in the Cevennes, where the poor peasants, led by their chiefs, held at bay the armies of Louis XIV. What France lost in this dire persecution, England gained, and many of the noblest natures have reflected their intelligence and religion on our own country.

Alison, the historian, remarks: " From the Revocation of the Edict of Nantes is to be dated the commencement of a series of causes and effects which closed the reign of Louis XIV. in mourning; indeed the weakness and disgrace of the French monarch spread the fatal poison of irreligion among the inhabitants, and finally overthrew that throne and that church which had made such an infamous use of their power."

Louis, at first moderate to the Protestants, afterwards became their oppressor. Long before 1685, cruel and unjust measures had been passed; their churches were destroyed, ministers forbidden to preach; while the system of depriving Protestants of all honours in the State,—and separation from their families, brought the severities of the Edict vividly before them.

Lady Rachel Russell writes in 1686: " 'Tis enough to sink the strongest heart to read the accounts sent over. How the children are torn from their mothers and sent into monasteries, their mothers to another, the husband to prison or the galleys."

A medal[3] commemorative of the event was struck, *Te Deums* were sung at Rome, and the greatest writers of the day eulogized the success of the "edict" which had been urged on the King by Madame de Maintenon and Père la Chaise, his confessor.

Robert Hall speaks of this period: "From the fatal moment when France put an end to the toleration of the Protestants, the corruptions of the clergy—the abuses of the church—the impiety of the people, met with no check till infidelity of the worst sort ruined the nation."

In the hair-breadth escapes to England and elsewhere, we read of thrilling incidents: the roads to the coast were watched by armed patrols—the ships in which the exiles sailed were often fumigated with deadly vapours, and the utmost cruelties were exercised on them, so that many who could not brave the dangers of transit abjured their faith for self-preservation, and then recanted on their arrival in England. So far was this the case, that it is related as a true occurrence of one who said, "J'ai damné mon âme, pour sauver mes biens."

[3] See illustration, page 73.

The long privations, the miseries of their dungeon life in some dismal fortress of the South, the cruel tortures and the weary days have been brightened by the heroic sacrifices made, as tale after tale repeated the noble efforts of wife, husband, or child for their mutual release or escape. These memoirs are often transmitted to us in the pages of historical romance, detailing many a thrilling incident of persecution and relief.[4]

The pamphlets of the time teem with the accounts of the fugitives, their number and circumstances; and it is recorded:[5] "They come hither in troops almost every day, the greatest part of them with no other goods but their children."

For some years after 1685, the influx of strangers continued. Not only London, but the seaports and manufacturing towns received them, and henceforth England really became their " home."

That nation quickly raised sums for their relief; free letters of denization were granted, and churches multiplied in all parts of the kingdom.

Events hastened on rapidly in the short years of James's reign; the Revolution of 1688 was

[4] "By Fire and Sword," a story of the Huguenots, by Thomas Archer. 1885.
[5] "Present State of the Protestants in France, 1681."

at hand, bringing with it those pioneers of right and truth, who in Church and State upheld the constancy, and softened the trials, of the suffering fugitives.

The landing of William of Orange on the 5th of November, 1688, at Torbay, brought with it important and lasting results.

In the relations of the refugees with William III. and his Irish campaigns another phase of history dawns on us, for Ranke observes:—
" Europe associated itself with English Protestantism in the Prince's army, and that in the most impressive way, by sending as its representatives the French refugees. They contended against the system which had driven them out of their country, and which now threatened, if it conquered in England, to subjugate the world. They were kept together by the universal feeling that the preservation of European freedom and of the Protestant religion depended on the success of this undertaking."

While contemplating their fidelity to the King's cause, the lines of Defoe, in his "Trueborn Englishman" are vividly recalled to us:—

"We blame the king that he relies too much
　On strangers, Germans, Huguenots, and Dutch;
　That foreigners have faithfully obey'd him,
　And none but Englishmen have e'er betray'd him."

The character of William is further drawn by Dr. Bersier, in his " Earlier Life of Coligny :"—"The conscience of man must have fallen low indeed, when the name of William of Orange ceases to be honoured. For the French Protestants the struggle was a terrible one, and fraught with dangers; but in sustaining it they deserved well of God and their country.

"Doubtless the cause they defended was often compromised by the ambition of its leaders, and we must deeply deplore the fact that in the conflict, the church sometimes became entangled with, and well-nigh merged into, a political party."

We shall revert to the efforts of the King in regard to the Royal Bounty Fund in another chapter. Meanwhile it is impossible to pass over the results of his Irish campaign, which enrolled in it such famous names as Schomberg, Ruvigny, Galway, and others. Nor is it too much to consider, that to these leaders, Protestantism in Ireland, owed its success.

Two leading prelates stand out prominently as the patrons and friends of the distressed strangers, viz. William Sancroft, Archbishop of Canterbury, and Henry Compton, Bishop of

London. Even in 1681, four years before the Revocation, we learn that the Privy Council recommended the Primate to write to the bishops of the Province of Canterbury to encourage contributions from the clergy and parishioners in aid of the foreigners.

The part Archbishop Sancroft took, as one of the "non-juring" prelates, made him liable to misconception, but his commendable frankness as regards the refugees, is related by his biographer, D'Oyly:[6]—

"Monsieur Du Bordieu, minister of the French Church in the Savoy, went to take leave of the Primate. His Grace told him that he did not doubt that the foreign Protestants would blame his conduct; but he declared that before he took that step he had foreseen even the injury which the part he took might do to the Protestant cause."

Bishop Compton's name recalls a close connection with this important period of our subject, as he held the See of London from 1675 to 1714. As tutor to the Princesses of Orange, it is alleged that their firm adherence to the Protestant faith was the result of this learned

[6] D'Oyly, "Life of Archbishop Sancroft."

man's guidance. John Evelyn, the diarist, often alludes to him, as a "most sober, grave, and excellent prelate." Compton aimed at promoting union among Protestants, and for that object invited the opinions of learned strangers, and corresponded with M. de L'Angle, one of the great preachers at Charenton, and with Monsieur Claude, another French divine. For his defence of the Protestant cause he was, on James' accession, suspended, but on the arrival of William III. regained favour.

So great was his furtherance of their interest, that it is said the refugees "drank deep of his bounty for many years; he maintained all along a brotherly correspondence with the foreign churches, and endeavoured to promote in them a good opinion concerning the doctrines and discipline of the Church of England."

It is a known fact that William of Orange obtained the aid of Parliament to grant a relief fund without much trouble; but the acts for naturalization were more difficult to get passed. The proceeding was unpopular with all boroughs and corporations, and did not become law till 1709. Meanwhile some few privileged persons obtained "royal letters patent."

Archbishop Tillotson succeeded Sancroft, and, along with Bishop Compton, greatly promoted the interest of the "strangers."

Another appeal was set on foot for contributions in the Diocese of London, at the instigation of that Primate, with successful results.

Bishop Lloyd held the See of Worcester at this time. We hear of him recommending the family of Mr. Bryenne, a French minister, to the Archbishop; and he wished to bring about a union between the Protestant churches and different states of Europe.

One eminent name is now conspicuous, and that is the Marquis Ruvigny, noted, not only on account of his connection by marriage with Lord William Russell, who was beheaded, but as associated with Ireland, over which country one of the family was Viceroy, and who was selected, on account of his friendship with the Russells, on a mission to England. The first Marquis, on coming here, settled at Greenwich, founded a congregation there, and was the leader of the foreign nobility in that place. His neighbour, one no less than John Evelyn, lived at Sayes Court, Deptford, and the diarist records a visit to the Marquis in 1685:—

"I went to visit the Marquess Ruvigné, now my neighbour at Greenwich, retired from the persecution in France. He was the deputy of all the Protestants of that kingdom in the Parliament of Paris, and several times ambassador in this and other courts; a person of great learning and experience." His son, Lord Galway, built churches at Portarlington, in Ireland, and exerted himself much for the refugees, by trying to induce Archbishop Tenison to get a settled fund for them from the government.

The illustrious Rachel, Lady Russell, whose memoirs are in every hand, was related to the Marquis Ruvigny, and thus a double interest is attached to the history of this nobleman.

In quitting the reign of William III., we notice, in his successor Queen Anne, a similar and zealous attachment for the welfare of the distressed people.

In 1703 the cause of the persecuted Cevennois aroused the just indignation of Europe, and the Queen sent messengers to France with her orders, and also commissioned certain refugee gentlemen to go aboard the English fleet, commanded by Admiral Shovel, in order to be witnesses of her intentions.

Boyer, the royal historian, informs us that in the year 1707 the ministers of the French churches in London and Westminster, by direction from the Bishop of Salisbury, met in the chapel of the Savoy, when Monsieur de la Rivière, one of their ministers, offered a thanksgiving for the victory of her Majesty's army, and for making her the instrument of restoration of the Protestant churches in France. To an address signed and presented, this significant reply was returned by the Queen :—

"I have always had great compassion for the unhappy circumstances of the persecuted Protestants of France; I will communicate my thoughts upon this matter to our allies, and hope such measures may be taken as may effectually answer the intent of your petition."

We read of several memorials to Parliament in this reign, for the better protection of the estates of the refugees, and for preventing subjects in France claiming the property of their relations, dying in England. The act which engrossed the greatest public interest was the Naturalization Bill, which did not pass till the year 1709.

Bishop Burnet spoke much for it, and the

Bishop of Chester (Sir W. Dawes) as zealously against the measure.

The Queen's care for her foreign subjects appears at no time to have diminished, and her answer, through Lord Dartmouth, to a petition of the principal French congregations in London to support their interests in the negotiation of peace in 1713 (the famous Peace of Utrecht) was as follows: " Her Majesty has so much consideration of your sufferings that she is willing to give any further directions that may be of advantage to you."

In the following year the Queen writes to Archbishop Tenison to make a collection for the " Society for the Propagation of the Gospel in Foreign Parts."

When we turn from the Queen to the church, we observe, during the next forty years, several Primates who carried out the same encouragement, and gave substantial assistance to the refugees as in former times. These were Archbishops Tenison, Wake, Herring, and Secker, who, by their patronage and correspondence, successfully combined with the government and the nobility for the desired end.

An example of this assistance is recorded in

the efforts of Archbishop Tenison, who, in 1696, on a petition of the Weavers' Company at Canterbury, was asked to promote the bill to restrict the importation of East India silks, and before that time Charles II. had granted a charter to enable the weavers to become a company.

The good principles which had formerly guided the exiles did not forsake them in their daily life. Of this special trait in their character we recall an incident of past times.[7] " An English gentleman was travelling through France, and in going through a valley his horse nearly ran over a child. He fell into conversation with the by-standers, and found they were Huguenots, and that they had with them a single copy of the Scriptures, with which they refreshed their faith. In going through the factory of the firm with which he had business, he inquired after these people. 'They are a silly sort of people, but we never have to weigh their silk, they brought their silk for sale, and their account was always received.' Although the world may call such a 'silly

---

[7] "Proceedings, Huguenot Society of America, 1883."

sort of people,' they are the bone and sinew and moral strength of any country."

Jurieu, in his *Lettres Pastorales* said truly, "The Protestants have carried commerce with them into exile," and the manufactures declined on their flight from France.

The influence of the English church was not only felt at home but abroad, in giving direction and support to many congregations in Germany, Holland, and Switzerland.

These measures were generally strengthened by the Government, and Jurieu, in writing to Archbishop Tenison, says that "the kings of England have been security, according to treatises and records, for the liberty of the Protestant churches of France." [8]

The co-operation of Dr. Wake is much interwoven with our subject, and his strenuous efforts to bring about a union between our own and the Gallican church of France, is an acknowledged point of history.

In earlier days, as chaplain to the British Embassy at Paris, Archbishop Wake had acquired great repute for learning and criticism,

---

[8] Lambeth MS. 953.

and carried on his long controversy with the Sorbonne on the much desired subject of union. In this correspondence, the Rev. W. Beauvoir, of refugee descent, and chaplain to the Earl of Stair (who was ambassador at Paris) comes before our notice. The family of De Beauvoir settled in Kent, and the Rev. Osmund Beauvoir one of the six preachers in Canterbury Cathedral, was master of the Free Grammar school there, and spoken of by Hasted, the Kentish historian, in high terms. It is supposed that De Beauvoir Town, Kingsland, takes its name from this family.

Returning to the subject of the Gallican church, Monsieur Dupin and three other doctors of the Sorbonne expressed their desire for union; but though at one time probable, it was not successfully concluded. Nevertheless, the letters and statements on this vexed question are transmitted to us and preserved in Christ Church, Oxford, where Archbishop Wake gave so many of his MSS. In the Lambeth collection, several papers, relating both to this point and to refugee churches, show how wide and enduring was the Primate's interest in these particular subjects.

It is also to be noticed that when Antoine Court, one of the famous preachers of the Cevennes, wished to found a college at Lausanne, he sought the aid of Archbishop Wake, whose interposition with George I. resulted successfully, and in 1729 the college was founded. The sentiments of the Primate may be best learnt from a sermon preached by him in 1699, on the occasion of a public fast—" It is but a little time since we were called on to receive those of the reformed church of France among us; by doing this, we have preserved so much of the Protestant interest from sinking; all that their persecutors have gained by their cruelty against them is this, they have forced them to change their country, but have not at all lessened their zeal for their religion or their ability to defend it."

Dr. Wake was a voluminous writer, and is best known by his "State of the Church," printed in 1703.

Reference was often made in these days to the contests which took place for church preferment, and this is exemplified by one of the satirical prints on which Horace

Walpole, in allusion to the vacant See, wrote:—

> "The man whose place they thought to take
> Is still alive, and still a-Wake."[9]

Archbishop Herring, who succeeded to the Primacy in 1747, responded warmly to the relief of persecution and distress, especially taking up the cause of the prisoners in the galley-ships. In many cases, this Prelate was associated with the Duke of Bedford for the suffering refugees in the Channel Islands.

Long was the correspondence which passed between the Archbishop, Lord Albemarle, Duke of Newcastle, and other noblemen who generally held influential positions abroad.

Lord Albemarle, writing from Paris, January, 1750, after referring to his endeavours with the French Government for the release of the slaves, says:[1]—

"Your Grace may be assured that my zeal for the cause, were not your recommendation a sufficient spur, will not let me miss the opportunity of renewing my application or discourage me in my pursuit, though out of the long list I

---

[9] Archbishop Wake.   [1] Lambeth MS., 1122.

gave formerly to the French ministry, I have only obtained the liberty of one of those poor people, whose name is François Farques."

Not only the French, but the distressed Protestants of Hungary and the churches in Germany received the Primate's support, and, perhaps, more than all, the Vaudois, whose name alone seems to recall many memories of the troubled history of those valley churches of Piedmont.

In his constant endeavours for the rescue of the galley slaves, Archbishop Herring obtained the aid of Holland. Other countries also extended the hand of friendship in the cause of truth and justice.

About this time, was founded the Society for encouraging Foreign Protestants, and the Rev. Jacob Bourdillon, minister of the Wood Street Chapel, Spitalfields, was the secretary in 1755.

In the establishment of a similar society in Ireland, we find Archbishop Herring in correspondence with the secretary, Monsieur Simon, and by the Primate's influence with the Lord-Lieutenant, aid was given to the numerous exiles who had settled in that country.

In no less warm manner did Archbishop Secker follow up the means for aid than his predecessors had done.

The ministers of Geneva had formed a relief fund, and the Primate's own words will best convey the expression of his feelings towards them :—

"It will always be a singular pleasure to me to assist you in this excellent undertaking, and to receive your advice and directions for that purpose; particularly the afflicted servants of God who suffer in France for the profession of the truth. "*September*, 1758." [2]

In the vexed question whether nonconforming French churches should share in the Royal Bounty equally with the conforming, this Prelate took a prominent part, and by his wise action often secured beneficial results.

As time progressed, the refugees became more prosperous and less in need of help, and the question of continuing the Royal Fund was agitated.

In this movement, Dr. Secker led the way by securing its continuance, as he himself says, "By mentioning it incidentally to the Duke of

[2] Lambeth MS., 1122.

Newcastle as a thing to be done of course, in which light he also considered it, and will accordingly represent it to his Majesty." Other measures were taken up by the Archbishop, who, with Lord Halifax, Lord Bute, Mr. Greville, Lord Egremont, corresponded with the King, often in a successful issue, either for money relief or for emigration to America, where lands were assigned the colonists.

A son of one of the most famous " Pastors of the Desert," as they were called, Antoine Court, writes to Dr. Secker, in 1761, on behalf of the people of the Cevennes; also that the Primate may recognize his succession as minister. He mentions the noted work of his father, " Histoire des troubles des Cevennes, ou de la guerre des Camisards," and begs leave to send a copy to the Archbishop.

In those rocky fastnesses of southern France, we can almost picture the assemblies worshipping for safety in the recesses of that vast district, the sky alone forming a canopy to their temple, while the words of their accustomed prayer would break the solemn stillness of the scene :—

"Eternel notre bon Dieu! Dieu du Ciel et

de la Terre, pour le service duquel nous souffrons tant de calamitez nous elevons nos yeux a toi, attendant ton secours, et ta delivrance. Seigneur, tu vois notre affliction, et notre dure servitude, Aye compassion de nous selon la grandeur de ta misericorde et la fidelite de tes promesses. Viens donc a notre secours, O notre bon Dieu. Campes tes Saintes Anges a l'entour de nos personnes, O toi, Seigneur Jesus qui es le chef des armées de l'Eternel, marche devant nous, conduis nous, protége nous, combat pour nous." [3]

"The Church in the Desert" thus became one of the most important agencies in France for the maintenance of religion; but even in those retreats, the congregations were persecuted and hunted down by their oppressors.

Towards the close of the eighteenth century, we happily learn that the tortures of the galleys and the prisons were beginning to decline. Liberty, however, had come too late for the exiles in England, and henceforth they were

---

[3] "Formulaire de Priere des Cevennois dans leurs assemblées." (Printed à Londres, par J. Delage dans Stationer-court, 1703.)

absorbed in the customs, speech, and society of their adopted land.

Although the cruelties have ceased, the weary want and privation is over, the refugees have become eminent and prosperous, yet the memory of those terrible times can never be effaced from France, while brighter recollections dawn, as the story of their lives centres in England.

(*See page* 54.)

CHAPTER IV.

French churches in LONDON—Their history—Rise and fall—Threadneedle Street Church—Its ministers—The Savoy and its services—Historical memories—Ministers—Somerset House Chapel—Durham House—The increase of churches in 1685—Spitalfields—Soho—The smaller churches—Dissension between the "Conformist" and other communities—Royal Bounty Fund and its history—Distinguished refugees in church annals — Allix — Casaubon — Colomiez — Jortin — Romaine—Famous names in Ireland.

AMONG the varied points of interest in refugee history, have been the churches established for worship in London and other parts of England. The countenance given to the Protestant exiles in the reign of Edward VI. and the appointment of John à Lasco as "superintendent" of their congregations, are two important data, to which reference has before been made.

Not the least historical among the buildings of "old London" was St. Anthony's Hospital in Threadneedle Street, which in the year 1485 was annexed to St. George's Church, Windsor. In 1550, leave was obtained from the Dean and Canons of Windsor that the chapel of this hospital be used for the French and Walloon service, and that proportionate payment should be made by these two bodies for the defrayal of rent and other expenses.

Thus, a footing was obtained for the free exercise of worship, and this was strengthened by the aid of Archbishop Cranmer, as appears by the following letter in the "Parker Society Publications," dated 1550. "Some of the bishops, and especially the Bishop of London (Ridley), are opposed to our designs. Archbishop Cranmer, the especial patron of the foreigners, has been the chief support and promoter of our church to the great astonishment of some."

It must be remembered that the earliest who frequented this church in Threadneedle Street were Walloons, who fled to England from the cruel tyranny of the Duke of Alva in the Low Countries, but that it gradually became the resort of both a French and Walloon congregation.

After the St. Bartholomew (1572), the great

tide of emigration rendered this the central place for worship; and indeed it may rightly be called "the cathedral" of the Huguenots.

The Fire of London laid this, like other buildings, in ashes.

In 1669 this church was rebuilt and opened, when its demolition in 1840, in order to make approaches for the Royal Exchange, caused the erection of the present church, about 1843, in St. Martin's-le-Grand, near the General Post Office. Thus, the Threadneedle Street edifice has had an important line of history. Here the refugees on their first arrival were wont to present themselves, and gain protection or redress as the case might be. Synods and meetings were also held, the first being in 1603, when ministers from various French and Dutch churches attended. Subsequent synods took place in 1634, 1641, 1644, and 1647.

Conferences to settle points of religion and doctrine met here. The Bishop of London was generally referred to for decision, and Grindal (afterwards Archbishop of Canterbury) figures among those who took great interest in this congregation. Grindal's enforced exile abroad, where he became acquainted with several learned men, gave him fuller sympathy with and knowledge of those who fled into England. This church was at times in great need, but in later days has become able to assist its poorer brethren. MSS. of documentary value, Acts of the Consistory, and various other records are here preserved; there is also a good collection of printed books on theology and history.

It is not surprising that men of note have been ministers of this congregation from its commencement in 1550. Several of them have been eminent for learning, while others were afterwards associated with the English church. "One of the earliest, Richard Vauville, called also Richard François, has been alluded to in a former chapter, and in the long succession of pastors, many call for remark. The early history of this church has also been recorded in the writings of English and foreign reformers. In 1621, one Jean Maximilien de l'Angle was minister, and the family became connected with the county of Kent.

His son was rector of St. George's, Canterbury, in 1683, and afterwards of Chartham, near that city, where he died in 1724.

Pierre Du Moulin, a name famous in Protestant history, was minister from 1624-31; his numerous works are noted, and "Le Bouclier de la foy," "Du Combat chrestien," are some of those which have earned for him great repute. His son was chaplain to Charles II. and rector of Adisham, in Kent, where he died 1685. Louis Herault, another of mark, was so zealous a Royalist, that he had to fly during the Commonwealth. On his return, he received a Canonry at Canterbury, and was buried in 1682 in that cathedral.

The name of Saurin is so known in refugee annals, that it recalls many works of piety and learning. Born at Nismes in 1677, he naturally acquired from that stronghold of Protestantism, earnest convictions—his ecclesiastical writings and sermons were numerous, and after preaching in London for about five years he went to the Hague to a congregation connected with the Prince of Orange. Saurin's name has become a bye-word in history, and the brothers were all noted. Louis was connected with the Savoy; he was afterwards Dean of St. Patrick's, Ardlagh, and his grandson became Bishop of Dromore. So great was

Saurin's eloquence that at Geneva, where he studied, the cathedral had to be opened to the crowd who flocked to him. He took Tillotson for his model, and it is said that when Abbadie heard him for the first time he said, " Is it a man or an angel who speaks ? "[1]

Later ministers of the Threadneedle Street church have maintained its excellence for scholarly fame and doctrine. Of them, Charles Butheau, who had been at the "Temple" at Charenton, near Paris, was conspicuous.

While noting only the most celebrated preachers, we must not omit the names of Durand, Romilly, Martin, Mercier, Bonnet, and others who, in this and the previous century, have maintained the succession of some sixty-three ministers since the foundation in 1550.

Before the Fire of London, there were only two or three foreign churches, of which the Savoy claims great and lasting interest. That Royal palace, whose walls were once washed by the silent Thames—that palace which has witnessed so many events in our kingdom—maintained within its precincts a service for the

---

[1] Weis's " Protestant Refugees."

Protestant faith. The "Savoy" has gathered round it such a train of incidents, that history would dwell long on those memories. The famous "Savoy Conference" was held here, and in the "Savoy House," as it was then called, Strype states there were "three or four churches and places for religious assemblies, viz., for the French, Dutch, High Germans, and Lutherans."

In Dr. Thomas Fuller, Chaplain, we record one who is well-known for his "Church History" and his "Worthies." Faithful and quaint in his discourses, his name will ever be linked with this building; and so humble was he of himself, that when asked to make an epitaph, he said, "Let it be, 'Here lies Fuller's earth.'"

From this digression, we come to the commencement of the French service in the hospital of the Savoy, in 1661, under the auspices of Sheldon, Bishop of London, and others, whereby what was called the Chapel ward was demised for the purpose, with the consent of the King, for a certain period of years.

In 1661, the first sermon was preached at

the Savoy, by Monsieur Jean Durel, minister. This discourse marks an historical and literary fact, as it had the official approbation of Dr. Sheldon to be printed, as expressed in these terms:—" Je ne trouve rien qui soit contraire à la foy, ou aux bonnes meurs, et qui empeche qu'il ne puisse estré imprimé pour utilité publique." 3rd Sep., 1662.

For nearly seventy years, French service was conducted here, increased by the arrival of exiles after the Revocation of the Edict of Nantes, so that the premises had to be enlarged.

About 1731, the chapel became in a ruinous condition, and the congregation migrated to Spring Gardens; also to what was called "Les Grecs" in Soho, until on its disuse and demolition, a new building was opened in Bloomsbury Street in 1845.

This church, called "L'église de St. Jean en Savoie" is the hereditary descendant, as it were, of the old Savoy, and thus a certain interest is gathered around its progress.

We must now revert to the fact that the Savoy congregation always conformed to the English liturgy, and that it had the support and patronage of the nobility, indeed it was the fashionable West End church.

Its ministers were of note and learning, from Jean Durel, the first pastor, in 1661, to David Durand in 1760. Among a succession of twenty, there are several whose names added a lustre to the roll. James Abbadie, minister about 1700, was present at the battle of the Boyne, where Marshal Schomberg fell. He drew large numbers to the Savoy, and even Madame de Sévigné, who did not espouse the Huguenot cause, said, "I do not believe that any one ever spoke of religion like this man."

His writings were powerful and numerous; his "Traité de la verité Chretienne," attracting most notice; they were translated into different languages, and are well known in Holland, where he afterwards lived. His attachment to the Royal cause was great, and showed itself in his defence of William III., and in a sermon on the death of Queen Mary. He was made Dean of Killaloe, and died in 1727.

The Rev. J. A. du Bourdieu was chaplain to three successive Dukes of Schomberg, also at the Savoy; at his instigation, Dr. Lloyd,

Bishop of St. Asaph, took up the cause of the persecuted Vaudois.

His sermons and treatises were many. On the occasion of the Marlborough victories, he likened Louis XIV. to a Pharaoh towards the oppressed Protestants. For this he was reprimanded; but on a representation, in 1713, before the Bishop of London, the matter was withdrawn.

The Rev. Claude de la Motte, who abandoned law for the Church, became minister of the congregation at Rouen in 1682, and then of the Savoy. An esteemed and voluminous writer, he also interested himself in the liberation of the galley-slaves.

David Durand, a very eloquent preacher, was born in 1699, and after many hair-breadth escapes for his life, fled to England from his native home in Dauphiny. An industrious author, he was engaged on a continuation of Rapin's "History of England;" was minister of the Savoy, about 1760. Some of his family were pastors of the French church at Canterbury, and the name of Durand has long lingered around that cathedral city and neighbourhood.

Old Somerset House, like the Savoy, is invested with many refugee memories, for in the chapel of that palace a French service was held, which Pepys, in 1664, thus notices,—" Thence to Somerset House, and there into the chapel, where Monsieur d'Espagne used to preach, but now it is made very fine, and was ten times more crowded than the Queen's Chapel at St. James's."

M. d'Espagne was the author of a work entitled, "Reformation de quelques passages de la Bible," and he was styled, "Ministre de St. Evangile," and is perhaps best known by his "Essay on the wonders of God," translated from the French. 1672.

The chapel was voted by Parliament, in 1653, for the use of the Protestants during pleasure, and in 1657 we read, " Ordered by his Highness, the Lord Protector, that it be recommended to the trustees for the maintenance of ministers to settle on M. d'Espagne, preacher at ye French congregation at Somerset House, an augmentation of 20*l.* per annum, for his better encouragement and maintenance."

We also learn that a service was held in the chapel of Durham House, one of the most historical sites of old London, inhabited by former Bishops of Durham, and granted by Queen Elizabeth to Sir Walter Raleigh.

The ground on which this ancient house once stood is now occupied by the "Adelphi;" it was, however, of Monsieur d'Espagne, preacher in the chapel there, that it is recorded, "his sermons were followed by many of the nobility and gentry," and that when Durham House was removed "it pleased God to promise us an order of the House of Peers to exercise our devotions at Somerset House chapel." It is a singular trait of those times, that this latter chapel, which had been erected for the Infanta of Spain about 1623, and afterwards used by Henrietta, Queen of Charles I., for the Romish ritual, should be granted for the simple and unadorned worship of French Protestantism!

After 1685 the number of foreign churches in London greatly increased, so that early in the eighteenth century thirty or more could be mentioned.[2]

[2] For lists and full descriptions of these and other churches, their ministers, &c., I must refer the reader to the works of Smiles, Weiss, and J. S. Burn.

In Spitalfields, the refugee stronghold, there were no less than nine, and among them, that of "La Patente," so called from the "letters patent" granted to the congregation in 1689, was the most important. Around "La Patente" gathered, as it were, several smaller places of worship, as in Crispin Street, Perle Street, also L'Église de l'Hôpital, afterwards L'Église Neuve, in Spitalfields. Some of these chapels had only a short term of existence; they afterwards united with the larger congregations, and some joined the London Walloon church in Threadneedle Street.

Amid all these changes, those firm traditions of the past were never forgotten by the fugitives in their "strange land;" the hymn that recalled the song of praise sung by their ancestors for fear of danger in some mountain fortress of southern France, re-echoed in these crowded London churches. The book that was read out aloud while others were hard at their weaving, spoke of the mental courage and suffering of their forefathers, who by that simple power of faith had braved persecution, and had transmitted the noble lesson of endurance to their children. At this time, the populous

Spitalfields district was more in the country than to-day; indeed, the very name implies an outlying part of London.

Some features of that period are still left, in Spital Square, the houses (once the abodes of the master silk manufacturers) have a substantial and old-world look; over the door heads, are carved canopies with brackets. Occasionally, one meets with the long glazed windows in the upper storeys, bespeaking the "weavers' halls," where the loom and the shuttle, with their busy click, told of the ceaseless occupation of the industrious exiles.

A street or two having a foreign name remains to tell the story of the past. In Spital Square once stood the pulpit cross, at which the celebrated sermons (now preached at Christ Church, Newgate), were delivered. The Bluecoat boys, in Elizabeth's reign, attended the sermons.

In views and maps of old London, we may discover the Fields as an open and partly wooded spot, rather different from the crowded streets of to-day!

Soho, the aristocratic London of the eighteenth century, was another resort of foreign

Protestants, and hence had many churches. Among the most famous was "Le Temple," once in Berwick, and then in Wardour Street, established in 1689. Around this could be traced out Glass House Street chapel, Golden Square, "La Charenton," in Newport Market, Leicester Fields Chapel, and many others.

There were also churches in or near Westminster, Piccadilly, Charing Cross, Hungerford Market. All have long ago disappeared; their sites can be occasionally traced by engravings[3] or old plans. A few retain their identity, but have been transferred to other denominations, as that of the Chapel Royal, St. James's, which, formerly called the Friary chapel, Pall Mall, had a French service, is now used for a German congregation. It may here be noticed, that Soho Square was begun in the reign of Charles II., and that in 1690, Evelyn records in his "Diary," "I went to London with my family to winter at Soho, in the great square." Several eminent men lived here, among them Bishop Burnet, whose interest in the refugees was undisputed.

[3] An instance of this occurs in Hogarth's famous picture of "Noon," in which the old chapel of "Les Grecs" (surviving in the present St. Mary, Crown Street, Soho) is depicted.

We now briefly revert to those ecclesiastical annals which have cast, so to speak, sunshine and shadow over these important and once numerous communities. It is impossible not to have found several dissentient elements in the constitution, teaching, and doctrines of these churches, and that the differences so arising should be submitted to an appeal or decision; the Archbishop of Canterbury or Bishop of London being the usual referees.

The two points which seem to have divided the feelings of the refugees were, on the question of adopting the conformist service (using the liturgy of the English Church, in French) or retaining the simpler and older forms of worship. The predilection generally shown for the conforming churches as participating in the Royal Bounty Fund, for the relief of the poorer congregations and their ministers, is not without comment.

The Bishops generally supported the conforming churches, and thus by their influence, aid was obtained, which in other ways would not have been forthcoming. This was rather different with William III., of whom it is said "that he opened in his own palace (Kensington) a French chapel, according to the confession of faith, the liturgy, and discipline *formerly in use in France*, which service was continued several years after Queen Anne's accession."

Much correspondence passed between the Archbishops and the ministers of the various London churches as to the recipients for the Royal Bounty Fund; perhaps that of Archbishops Herring and Secker with Mr. Majendie most aptly illustrates the point in question. Mr. Majendie was minister of the Savoy Church in 1747, and we read of a memorial from it and its dependent chapels, presented to Archbishop Herring for the purpose of aid.

It is also recorded that Mr. Majendie wrote to Archbishop Secker on a difficult question as regards the appropriation of pensions to conforming or nonconforming congregations, and whether the latter were entitled to pensions? The matter for some years caused much diversity of opinion, and petitions from the several churches—conformist, and of the old faith—were sent in, signed by the ministers and elders of the said congregations.

The history of the Royal Bounty Fund is also a leading episode of the time, and may here be briefly sketched. The royal annuity seems to have originated in the reign of Charles II., and some of the proceeds were divided equally among the preaching ministers of the Savoy. It was, however, William III. who got Parliament to grant 15,000*l.* annually for relief; and he spoke, on the 22nd of November, 1695, to the effect that, " Compassion obliges me to mention the miserable circumstances of the French Protestants who suffer for their religion."

When the elections came on at Westminster for the King's cause, the refugees there worked incessantly for their Royal patron, and so returned their gratitude. This fact nullifies the objections often made, that the Huguenots were disloyal to Church and State : it was the treatment and attitude of certain prelates that forced upon them a change of action.

A clerical and lay committee was appointed to adjudicate on the relief fund, and the lists of applicants were carefully supervised by those in authority. Though, as far as possible, justice was done in the distribution, yet many accusations were rife of alleged inequality of aid. These grievances found their way into the press, and formed the motive for several pamphlets of the day, especially one styled "Preuves des malversations et des injustices du Commité François dans l'administration des charitez publiques." As a rejoinder to this, we find another called, "Relation dans laquelle on fait voir l'établissement des bureaux et des distributeurs" (without name), 1705. The wrongs and rights of the mode of relief are impossible to discuss here; suffice to say, that they appeared in the literature of the time, and are important data as giving names and other valuable notes for the historical student. As time progressed, and the refugees became prosperous, the need for aid was not so urgent, the Bounty Fund was diminished, and before the death of George I. it was reduced to about 8500*l.* annually. There were, however, cases which demanded assistance, and thus the fund was drawn upon in excess.

The French Protestants of Exeter sent a petition through their Bishop (Lavington) to Archbishop Secker in 1760, that the small sum granted them may be increased, that they may support a minister properly. The signatures attached to this document are, locally, very interesting. Other petitions from some of the London churches were of frequent occurrence; one instance being of Castle Street, and Berwick Street, Westminster, where, in consequence of voluntary contributions having so much decreased, appeal was made for a part of the Royal Bounty. Again, Monsieur Barnouin, the minister at Southampton asks for aid: this is supported by Bishop Hoadly, of Winchester, who promotes the case in higher quarters.

The latest definite effort to continue the Bounty Fund was made by Archbishop Secker, who writes to Mr. Majendie, 7th of November, 1760:[1]—

"Sir,—I have taken the most effectual way of securing the continuance of H.M. Bounty to our Protestant brethren at home and abroad, by mentioning it incidentally to the Duke of Newcastle as a thing to be done of course. . . .

"The Duke, I am sure, is sincerely our friend as the King, God be thanked, takes pleasure in everything that is good, so that is a matter free from all difficulty ; no merit can be obtained by
"Your loving brother,
"Tho. Cant."

The friendship which existed between Arch-

[1] Lambeth MS., 1122.

bishop Secker and Mr. Majendie is seen in the long correspondence on the subject of relief to the various Protestant causes at home and abroad.

Of some twenty French churches in London, about 1730, not more than half were in existence towards the close of the century, so that their later accounts are necessarily limited and meagre.

From the intercourse of the English and foreign communities, it is not surprising that many noted names are enrolled on the page of history—names that have intertwined themselves round our own annals, and have shed a lustre through the sufferings of their ancestors, a lustre deepened by that Faith which arose from an earnest conviction of truth in Scripture.

From several of the refugees can be traced divines, authors, and writers who exercised a wide influence on the spirit of the age. Mr. R. S. Poole, in his "Huguenots of the Dispersion," says,—" It is the laborious vigour of the Huguenot personality which colours most strongly the literature of the refugees."

Among some of the more distinguished may be selected Peter Allix, once minister at Charenton, an appointment which generally followed on literary merit. Charenton, as before stated, was the great Protestant temple of France, and on its destruction, in 1685, a Benedictine monastery was built on the site. On coming to England, Allix produced a work called "Reflections on the Scriptures," dedicated to James II., and this seems to have been a stepping-stone to his advancement. We find him also connected with one of the Spitalfields churches. As a writer and scholar, he was the incessant adversary of Bossuet, and the advent of William III. brought forth many pamphlets from his pen. He was much engaged in controversial theology—on the Trinitarian doctrine; his Hebrew scholarship was great. He received a degree of D.D. from both Universities, and in 1690, through the kindness of Bishop Burnet, was made Treasurer and Canon of Salisbury Cathedral. His son became Dean of Ely, and the family have settled in the East of England.

Isaac Casaubon's name recalls much that has a claim to learning and piety, as well as connection with the English church. One of the earlier refugees, he will be remembered as escaping to England after the fatal St. Bartholomew—James I. afterwards befriended him, and made him a Prebend of Westminster. His son Meric, invites even a longer consideration, and the romantic episode that while hiding in a cavern from his persecutors, he learnt from his father his first Greek lessons, is no less remarkable than true. Entering at Christ Church, Oxford, Meric Casaubon became distinguished for his learning, and finally rose to a Prebend of Canterbury Cathedral and Rector of Ickham in Kent. A monument in that noble minster, and a bequest of MSS. to the library there, associate him in an especial degree with our own church and its annals.

Charles Marie Du Veil, D.D., was a refugee in England in 1677. He renounced Roman Catholicism and was ordained a minister of the Church of England. In his "Commentary on Matthew and Mark" he made a retractation of all his Romish arguments.

On becoming an Anabaptist, all his friends forsook him, except Archbishop Tillotson; this occurred, though he had received high encomiums from Bishop Lloyd (St. Asaph), Bishop Burnet (Salisbury), and Simon Patrick, Dean of Peterborough, afterwards Bishop of Ely.

Paul Colomiez, grandson of the great preacher of that name at La Rochelle, has left his mark on the seventeenth century writers and divines in England. Appointed by Archbishop Sancroft as his librarian,[5] he was the author of several learned works; and finally collated by that primate to the vicarage of Eynsford in Kent.

Sancroft chose chaplains and others about him for their excellence and learning, of whom Henry Wharton, so well known to historical scholars, was the most eminent.

As a theologian and literary worker, Dr. Jortin, Archdeacon of London, will be familiar to many, especially for his "Life of Erasmus."

The son of a Brittany refugee, Dr. Jortin achieved distinction at Cambridge, and was engaged by Pope on his translations of Homer. As Vicar of Kensington and Archdeacon of London, he was brought into contact with many noted men, and attracted the attention of Archbishop Herring, who gave him the living of St. Dunstan's-in-the-East. It is related that Dr.

---

[5] The other librarians of refugee descent, were Hans de Veille, and Dr. Ducarel, author of "Anglo-Norman Antiquities," and other works.

Jortin, dining at the Festival of the Sons of the Clergy, could not find his hat to go to the primate, who had sent for him. Then and there, the doctor was presented with the living of St. Dunstan's, and he returned, saying, "I have lost my hat, but I have got a living." It appears Dr. Jortin was afterwards Vicar of Eastwell in Kent, and the neighbouring living of Westwell is now held by the Rev. H. H. d'Ombrain, whose ancestors escaped from France in an open boat, in the sixteenth century.

The Rev. W. Romaine, a popular London clergyman in the middle of the last century, was an M.A. of Oxford, and had for his contemporary the famous Whitfield. His "Life, walk, and triumphs of Faith" is his best known book; his preaching was eloquent and vigorous; of Huguenot origin, and also connected with the English church, his name is well known and honoured.

Ireland claims some eminent refugees, either in the church, literature, or science, and although my subject bears on their life in England, there are close connections with the Sister country.

Many circumstances led to the arrival there of the followers of William III.; the industries of Cork, Limerick, and Waterford held out great resources.

In Ulster, others were attracted by a very natural circumstance, viz., the settlement of the Scotch Covenanters, a common cause in religion and suffering would make common friends. In Ireland, as in England, foreign Protestantism was strengthened by the aid of the English Church; at Waterford and Portarlington, large congregations were formed.

In 1674, the Parliament in Dublin passed an act for letters of naturalization, and the Duke of Ormond, Viceroy of Ireland in the reign of Charles II., countenanced the movement.

Fleury is a family much associated with Ireland; from Louis Fleury, pastor of Tours, who fled in 1683, was descended the Rev. G. L. Fleury, who became Archdeacon of Waterford.

Another, known in literature, and famous for heroism in danger, was De Bostaquet, who, possessed of large estates in Normandy, had to fly for his life, and afterwards, by great perils, reached Holland, the Protestant asylum of the north, where he was engaged in the service of William of Orange, whom he accompanied to England and Ireland. De Bostaquet was connected with the French church at Portarlington, and the records of his life were made use of by Lord Macaulay in his "History of England."

These papers became the property of Dean Vignoles, of Ossory, of whose family we can here speak. Coming from Languedoc, this name has been illustrious; several members entered the army, and some the church, of whom I may instance the Rev. John Vignoles, minister at Portarlington (1793—1817); his son succeeded him, and eventually rose to be Dean of Ossory.

Another name in Irish annals was Pierre Drelincourt, son of the excellent pastor, C. Drelincourt, author of more than forty different publications. This son Pierre, at first a refugee minister in England, afterwards became Dean of Armagh.

In the realm of history, Rapin is a household word, and yet few perhaps connect him with the soldier-writer who figured so bravely in

William III.'s army at the Battle of the Boyne, and who was wounded at the siege of Limerick. His intelligence and learning brought him under the special notice of the King, and he was selected as tutor to the Duke of Portland's son. This appointment caused residence abroad, chiefly at the Hague, where he wrote his history, founded on Rymer's "Fœdera," a work on which he was engaged for seventeen years.

Fontaine, or De la Fontaine, is a representative name for a family who underwent great risks in their flight to England and elsewhere; Jacques Fontaine was minister at Cork, in 1695.

"Scholars of the refuge" may be justly applied to these learned men, who engrafted some of that ' Celtic *verve* and enthusiasm on our opinions and literature. One name, honoured and familiar to us in the person of Archbishop Trench, of Dublin (resigned), claims twofold refugee ancestry in the families of Chenevix and Trench.

The former, Chenevix, fled at the Revocation into England, and a descendant became Bishop of Killaloe, and afterwards of Waterford and Lismore about 1745. The latter, Tranche, or La Tranche, was a fugitive, after St. Bartholomew, first in Northumberland, and then in Ireland. One, Power Trench, was the last Archbishop of Tuam, and died in 1839. The members of both families have been distinguished in the church, state, and science.

While these short notices have been restricted to those famous in the church, we cannot ignore others who, in the army, navy, art, and letters have achieved distinction.

To all who desire fuller information, the ample biographies in the pages of Smiles, Weiss, or Agnew should be consulted. Many a worker in the humbler crafts has laboured for the better skill and practice of them in England, so that the tribute given to the influence of the refugees by an eminent American writer [6] is not without weight: "The virtues, accomplishments, and the arts which France lost by the banishment of its most conservative element, brought the blessings which France rejected, to the nations who received her exiles."

[6] The Hon. John Jay, address, "Huguenot Society of America," 1883.

CHAPTER V.

Suburban congregations—Provincial churches—Rye, Dover, Sandwich, Maidstone, Faversham, Southampton, the Channel Isles—Religious differences—The West of England—East Anglia—Canterbury and the Crypt Church—Archbishop Tait's encouragement of—Present condition—Historical and refugee names round Canterbury—Its ancient aspect and memories.

OF the suburban churches devoted to refugee worship, the most interesting, historically speaking, was Greenwich,—for there, the little circle of distinguished exiles had been formed by the aged Marquis de Ruvigny. Related to the Countess of Southampton, and uncle to Lady Russell, the Marquis gathered around him a two-fold interest in many ways. The congregation seems to have met in the parish church, as noticed by John Evelyn, who in 1687 says, "At the conclusion of the Church service, there was a French sermon preached after the use of the English liturgy, translated into French, to a congregation of about 100 refugees, of whom the Marquis Ruvigny was the chief, and had obtained the use of the church after the parish service was ended."

This settlement, founded by the Marquis in 1686, appears to have dispersed about 1718; but inscriptions in the churchyard, and various entries in the registers, fully attest the survival of many foreign families.

In the former, occur the names of Sir John Lethieullier, who died 1718, also John Savary, 1795, and Anthony William Boehm, who is called a "refugee." The register of the present parish church (St. Alphage) contains marriages of Frenchmen soon after the year 1685, and it seems that a chapel existed for their worship, but was taken down when the Greenwich railway was made.

It is difficult to reconcile Evelyn's statement as to service in the (parish?) church with that of a separate building, which must have been used or erected after the period mentioned by him.

At Wandsworth, a congregation was established so early as 1573; the chapel was enlarged in 1685, and repaired in 1809.

The first arrivals here were Flemish, about 1572; or, as described by Aubrey, the Surrey historian, there was a "manufacture of brass plates for kettles, frying-pans, &c., by Dutchmen, who keep it a mystery." The next, in 1685, were French, who followed the occupation of dyeing, hat-making, &c., and who enlarged this chapel as above mentioned, and to the end of the last century, the service was performed in French. The building was used by the Independents, and what remains is situate in an obscure locality, almost facing the parish church. Near at hand, is the cemetery called "Mount Nod," where many a refugee inscription can be traced; this historical spot has been made more known by an account having been printed in a pamphlet form, and by its better preservation. Among the more prominent persons are mentioned M. Baudoin, who fled from France in 1685, Vanderhoven, Dormay, Montolieu, Grosse, and many others. This quiet resting-place, surrounded by luxuriant trees, is indeed one of the "hallowed spots of London," and in visiting it we recall the lines of the poet Webster,—

> "I do love these ancient ruins.
> We never tread upon them, but we set
> Our foot upon some reverend history."

At Hammersmith, where another settlement existed, there appears to have been a church, and foreign names occur in the register. In 1703, one Mr. Bernard Rechou was minister; among those to whom the Royal bounty was extended, occurs the name of Monsieur Mazars, the pastor, in 1706.

The enthusiast must not limit his searches to districts once exclusively foreign; he may find all round the suburban parishes, traces of refugee life and memorials, as evidenced in the fact of Jean Cavallier, the great Camisard leader, having died at Chelsea, and been buried in the old (St. Luke's) churchyard there.

In the provinces, we find large settlements, chiefly on the south-east and western parts of England. At Rye, an early congregation was formed, at the first of many Flemish who came to this, and the adjoining Kentish coast.

As the nearest port to France, Rye attracted several fugitives; it was also a favourable place for the despatch of troops when England assisted the French Protestants in their wars.

Like other towns receiving refugees, it had an influx at three successive periods, viz., in 1568, 1572, and 1685.

In 1568-69 the Civil war in France caused a migration, and lists of those who fled to Rye, and were resident there, can be found in the Cottonian MSS. in the British Museum; among them were some ministers; and of the lay population many came from Rouen and Dieppe.

After St. Bartholomew (1572) we read that 647 persons had entered this town, and in 1583 the numbers were 1534. In 1586 the State papers record that the ministers of the French church are in communication with Sir Francis Walsingham; they desire letters to the magistrate, where they shall take up their abode.

The increase of strangers led to a proposal for the removal of several from Rye, and after the year 1590, the numbers lessened considerably.

In 1587 conferences of the French churches were held here, but soon after that time the members had so much decreased that Monsieur Morel, the minister, reported he must leave, for want of means; a "colloque," or assembly, had been held at Canterbury, on this and other matters of church government.

In James I.'s reign there was a small foreign population, but as we approach the time of the

"Revocation of the Edict of Nantes," a great increase took place, as is seen by the mayor's report contained in the "State papers" as follows:—"1681-88. 'These are to certifie all whom it may concerne, that the French Protestants who are settled inhabitants of this town of Rye are a sober, harmless, innocent people, such as serve God constantly, according to the usage and custom of the Church of England; and further, that we believe them to be falsely aspersed for Papists and disaffected persons. April 18th, 1682. Signed by the authorities of the town.'"

In 1685 it is stated that the captains of vessels between Rye and the French coasts made returns of the passengers they brought over.

The inhabitants declared their willingness that these Protestants newly-settled there might continue their assemblies in the English church, and have the use of the pulpits and seats, &c. From 1682 to about 1727 there were many settlers at Rye; after that time the numbers declined, and the history of the refugees merged into that of the ordinary inhabitants.

We learn that at their first coming, the old chapel of the Augustine Friars was supposed to have been their place of worship, and that afterwards they had the use of the parish church.

The names of the first ministers are difficult to identify; a few come before us and serve to mark a period of history.

In 1572, one Monsieur Michell; in 1583, Louis Morel, who came from Southampton; afterwards the name of Gébon, which ultimately became Gibbon. The books of this congregation have been lost, so that it is only by scattered documents we can gain occasional information.

The funds for maintenance were very poor; the appeals of Monsieur Bennoch, the pastor, and Monsieur Campredon, at Dover, to Archbishop Tenison, in 1697, set forth the grievance of inadequate allowance to maintain the proper service.

The sum which was to have been allowed does not seem to have been regularly paid, as Mr. Deffray intercedes with the Archbishop. He states their churches are composed of very poor families, and that unless some help is obtained, the ministers will be discouraged to continue in their present situation. The Lambeth MS. 1029 gives these particulars at greater length.

"Refugees in Sussex" might well form a theme of note, for from early times, Rye and Winchelsea welcomed their arrival, and it cannot be doubted that the first impetus given to their settling here, was the industries of the cloth and iron trade in the bordering towns of Kent. Foreign names, though in altered guise, have long survived, and of these may be cited the Le Telliers, who have become Taylors, and that of Dansay—connected with George I., who, when driven by stress of weather in 1725 into Rye, one Dansay, captain of a trading vessel, had the honour of bringing the King on shore. This quaint old town, though bereft of its once foreign colony, retains a primitive appearance. The narrow streets, with overhanging houses, the massive Ypres Tower serving as a kind of guard and outpost, the sluggish river, and the winding harbour, all point to a tale of the past, when this place was alive with the commerce and influence of several nations.

To quote a modern writer, "We breathe the very air of the past in these antique streets, up and down, hither and thither, roughly paved, with many a gabled house here and there, and strange ruins, and gates, and towers."

Mr. Basil Champneys, in his "Corner of England," speaks of Rye as having "in its general aspect at least the strangeness of a foreign town, and its individual remains are certainly not less interesting. There are many old streets to explore, houses having frowning story over story, which promise a wealth of the picturesque."

At Dover are distinct traces of immigration, that port being naturally, one of frequent and important service.

An early arrival was in 1621, when, on account of the troubles, "French Protestants daily land at Dover;" some ministers desiring the use of the parish church on certain days, request Lord Zouch to apply to Archbishop Abbot on their behalf. The Primate wished to have a return of the number of the communicants and non-communicants of foreign birth. It is probable that the strangers were allowed the use of the parish church of St. Mary's, the State papers[1] recording that the French in 1621 had service there three times a week. A regular congregation was formed in 1646, and one Phillippe le Keux was their minister; in 1634, Etienne Payenne; and in 1719, Jean Campredon.

Names of foreign lineage in the adjoining parishes attest the refugee element; there are found those of Tournay, Delancy, Minet, and others around Dover, while the family of Papillon from Avranches have at different times represented the ancient borough in Parliament. In this part of Kent land was sometimes given for the maintenance of the French services both at Canterbury and elsewhere, and the donors were generally of foreign descent. In no neighbourhood does there appear to have been so large a number of English clergy of refugee origin as the district around Dover. At Sandwich the Walloons, in the reign of Elizabeth, settled, and probably used one of the parish churches for their service; that Queen also granted them liberty to exercise their manufactures.

Archbishop Parker on his visit here in 1563

---

[1] Domestic series, James I.

spoke of them as "profitable and gentle strangers which ought to be welcome and not grudged at." Many trades were carried on, and some names remain, even to this day, which proclaim a long inherited and foreign lineage. St. Clement's was one of the churches allowed for use, on payment of a small annual sum or a portion of the repairs. During Laud's primacy, 1634, occurred the appeal of the ministers of the Dutch churches at Sandwich and Maidstone against the imperative demands of the Archbishop towards a conformity to the English liturgy and church government. Many, rather than lose their independency of worship, left the place; the matter, however, was interrupted by the Civil war, but survives in literature in a pamphlet by John Bulteel, minister of the Walloon church at Canterbury, entitled "The troubles of the three foreign Churches in Kent."

At Hythe, another Cinque port, can be traced some foreign families who once represented that place in Parliament; those of the Desbouveries and Huguessens being of local importance.

Of Faversham and Maidstone there is but

slight record of refugee settlements; though at the former town some foreign names remain, that of Giraud having long held honourable repute. There is but slight evidence of a church here, although towards the end of the seventeenth century we read of French ministers who officiated. At Maidstone, the Dutch and Flemings settled in 1573 under the protection of Queen Elizabeth, and were allowed to retain their own service, the corporation having granted them St. Faith's Chapel and burial-ground. The same stringent measures were adopted here as at Sandwich by Archbishop Laud, and the result of his policy was the dispersion of the foreign residents.

Freedom of worship was resumed under the Commonwealth; we can find little or no trace of French families at Maidstone, and the large numbers of Dutch may, in a measure be attributed to the demand for cloth-weaving, spinning, &c., the workers in which formed a guild for the protection of their interests in this town.

The history of the Southampton congregation, at first for the Walloons, and afterwards for joint service with the French, is much interwoven with the policy of the English church, and especially with Bishop Horne, of Winchester. That Prelate used his influence with Cecil (Lord Burleigh) for the Walloons in 1567, by gaining them the "Domus Dei" at Southampton, and also permission to exercise their trades. The visitor may now see near the partly-standing walls of this ancient town the church formerly called "God's House," or the chapel of St. Julian. Founded in the reign of Edward III. it was used by the Walloons in the time of Edward VI., and in a measure has remained intact, though greatly altered by modern repairs.

The registers are said to be the best preserved of such documents. The members adopted the conformist rite as at Norwich and Canterbury; several dissensions arose on this point on the arrival of the Huguenots after the St. Bartholomew. The history of the Southampton church naturally leads to that in the Channel Islands, with which it was ecclesiastically connected.

The foreign colonies in these Isles might well form a chapter by itself, and they have been much intermixed with our own history. The late Victor Hugo graphically describes their position as "Ces morceaux de la France, tombés dans la mer et ramassés par l'Angleterre."

Many circumstances led to their close connection with England and France, their position naturally made them a safe retreat; and from the time of Edward VI. we may trace the rise and progress of Protestantism, not unchecked by persecution and severity. The governors of the islands have had more or less influence in church affairs; one of the earliest was the Duke of Somerset, in the reign of Edward. The Book of Common Prayer, translated into French, and printed in 1553, "Pour les isles de sa Magesté," has already been noticed.

In the publication of this book, the Duke advocated the cause of the French printing-press with the King. During Queen Mary's reign, in the Channel Islands, as elsewhere, persecution raged, and we can chronicle nothing.

Under Elizabeth much progress was made, and the Huguenots petitioned for the use of their religion in all the churches of Jersey. The Queen, with a wisdom habitual to her policy, only allowed it at the parish church of St. Helier.

In 1564, the first Synod held at Guernsey

decreed to send a delegate to the Bishop of Winchester, and long afterwards that See (formerly attached to Coutances) has played a leading part in the refugee history of the islands. Several illustrious names have appeared as governors of Jersey or Guernsey. Of the former was Sir Walter Raleigh in 1600; the right of nomination to livings was vested in the governor.

During the sway of Sir John Peyton, we hear of discussions as to the obligations to conform to Episcopal jurisdiction, which was much exerted in Jersey and Guernsey. The nomination by the above-named governor of one who had received ordination at Oxford, to be a minister of the French Church, created indignation.

The "colloquy" resented this movement, but eventually yielded to what might be called a breaking away from the traditions of the Huguenot faith. The Islands, in a great measure, adopted the "conforming" system, which was supported by the English church.

James I. continued the like privileges to the refugees, as Elizabeth had done; but owing to some opposition to the orders that Queen had made, Archbishop Abbot reserved the office and authority of the Dean of Jersey, and ordered that the Book of Common Prayer should be reprinted in French, and used in the island churches, but that the ministers should not be bound to it in every particular.

In 1610 we hear of the enactment of "Canons Ecclésiastiques," and that the work of reconstituting them was placed in the hands of Archbishop Abbot, Bishop Montague (London), and Bishop Williams (Winchester).

The result of the change was a great modification of system among the congregations, and conformity, acknowledging the King as the head, became general.

The Commonwealth in this, as in other districts, produced a freer opinion on religious matters, and during its sway, the Channel Islands returned to their earlier and simpler forms of worship. This, however, was quickly extinguished on the Restoration in 1660, and the Act of Uniformity soon afterwards, completely reduced the churches to their former episcopal government. This Act was not without its consequences, several foreign ministers, rather than adopt Anglicanism, gave up their livings, and thus great variance was created.

Guernsey retained a more Calvinistic feeling than the other islands, having imbibed much of the Genevese doctrine, but this was quickly abandoned on the return of the monarchy.

In 1673, Jean de Saumarez was Dean of Jersey, and it is recorded that during his rule, strict adherence to the conforming system was absolute, indeed it is impossible to conceal that the influence of James II., in a great degree promoted these measures.

About 1700, Bishop Trelawney of Winchester, gave attention to the Isles and their government; the "Canons Ecclésiastiques" again enforced, caused much discord, especially from one of the ministers, Monsieur Picot, of Torteval in Guernsey. Correspondence passed between him and Bishops Mews and Trelawney which revealed the new position of the foreign ministers in their relation to the English church.

The authority of the Dean as affecting refugee worship was, at times, unduly exercised, and hence the appeal of their churches to the Primate or Bishops, and among those who supported their cause were Drs. Tenison (Canterbury), and Hoadly (Winchester).

About 1750 we find Archbishop Herring interesting himself with the Duke of Bedford for the relief of the Jersey exiles; some pecuniary aid was obtained till a certain number could be transported to other countries.

Thus, to an almost recent period we hear of the Church of England, along with the nobility, doing her share to help those, who, though differing in creed, must acknowledge one universal faith. Through all the changes in the Channel Isles, the foreign ministers have perhaps clung more tenaciously than elsewhere to their own tenets, and conformity to Anglican rites, had at times, a hard battle to succeed.

In the West of England, large settlements were made at Bristol, Barnstaple, Exeter, Plymouth, Dartmouth, &c., and consequently churches existed in those places, the exiles arriving being chiefly from La Rochelle, Brittany, Nantes, &c.

At Bristol, after the Revocation of the Edict of Nantes (1685), their congregation first assembled in the chapel of the Hospital of St. Mark's, otherwise called "Gaunt's Hospital," which they retained till the year 1721, when they erected a building for their own use.

The Episcopal jurisdiction which they retained, brought them in contact with some noted men.

In the carrying on their service, the aid of Bishop Trelawney of Bristol, and of the mayor and magistrates of that city, is much to be noticed.

Trelawney will be remembered as one of the seven bishops sent to the Tower; the loyalty of the Cornish miners in coming to the rescue of their countryman is perpetuated in the famous ballad—

> "And shall Trelawney die?
> Twenty thousand Cornish men
> Will see the reason why!"

The congregations were at first full to overflowing; about 1790 a great decline was visible, and in 1814 ceased altogether.

At Plymouth and Stonehouse, the foreign immigration took place at the end of the 18th century, and the services for both towns appear to have been held in the same building. Occasionally the registers of the parish church of St. Andrew's, Plymouth, contain a record of refugee births and baptisms from about 1689 to 1741.

"The good folk of Barnstaple," said Jacques

Fontaine, who had escaped there in an English ship (1685) "showed themselves full of compassion in our regard, they made us welcome in their homes and entreated us with affectionate care."

At Exeter, the community was formed soon after 1685, and one of the parish churches was granted for service. The names of Bishop Lavington, Mr. Majendie, and Archbishop Secker occur most frequently in connection with this church, to which reference is made in Chapter IV. Most of these West of England towns can be associated with William of Orange, whose landing, with his followers at Torbay, would naturally aid the Protestant cause. De Bostaquet, one of his generals, attended service while at Exeter in the Cathedral, and was much astonished at the ritual of the time (James II.), and said, "All this is very much opposed to the simplicity of our reformed religion."[2]

The tapestry manufacture at Exeter employed many artizans, who formed part of the congregation there.

[2] "Mémoires inédits de Dumont de Bostaquet."

In Eastern England, a large and important colony was founded, of which Norwich was the most famous.

The Dutch and Flemish had been the first to establish a manufacture of worsted stuffs; indeed, so early as the reign of Edward II. Norwich was very famous for that industry. In 1564 the trade was at a very low ebb, and it was resolved to invite the strangers of the Low Countries who had been driven away by Alva's persecution. Thus was provided, a good source of employment, so that towards the end of the 16th century there were over 3000 strangers in the place.

Queen Elizabeth, though willing to give them all protection, provided they conformed to the ecclesiastical and civil government of the city, commanded that the mayor and his officials should institute an inquiry as to their number, their attendance at any service, &c.

The early history of the Norwich congregation is much connected with what is called the "Discipline of the Walloon Church," which forms one of the leading features of the Reformed faith in the 16th century.

It may here be stated, that the foreign

churches each had their own code or form of "discipline" based on the same general principles, though differing in detail, the articles having been drawn up and approved by the minister, elders, and deacons.

That of London, brought out under the eye of John à Lasco, who was "Superintendent" of all the foreign churches, was the original and leading code.

We learn Canterbury had its form, but in that of Norwich great interest centres for many reasons.

In 1589 the French congregation had become so important that they also adopted their own "discipline," particulars of which are fully described in the "Norfolk Antiquarian Miscellany," (vol. ii.), by Miss Toulmin Smith. The Norwich document is increased in value by having the signatures of the ministers and elders attached, thus forming, with that of London and Canterbury, one of the most important records.

The place of worship allowed, both for the Walloons and French, was at first, the Bishop of Norwich's chapel, afterwards one of the city churches.

We follow almost the same events here as at Canterbury, the divisions between the Conformist and non-Conformist sections, the mediation of some of the Bishops, and their course of action. In most of these changes, the Mayor and corporation took their part in advice or co-operation.

During the continuance of the congregation, it became possessed of property near Norwich; but on the dissolution of the church, about 1820, a scheme was provided for dispensing the funds to charitable purposes, in which the French Protestant Hospital in London was entrusted.

The ministers of this church have been more or less noted by their works or their circumstances to merit mention, and among some twenty, since the foundation, may be selected Monsieur Basnage, Peter de Laune, Jean Bruckner, and others.

To this day, refugee families exist in or near Norwich, showing what an important settlement it must have been, as still seen in the well-known names of Martineau, Desormeau, Columbine, Mottram, &c.

Another spot was Thorney Abbey, in Cambridgeshire, where a congregation was formed in 1652, which lasted seventy-five years.

It is no less interesting than remarkable to state, that the once vast lands of this noted monastery became the abode of several Protestants from North Holland, who were afterwards increased by those from France. The possession of this property by the Russell family claims remark, as it is a matter of history that one of the Dukes of Bedford took up earnestly the cause of the exiles in the eighteenth century.

In the churchyard at Thorney are several inscriptions; a transcript of foreign names in the registers in a work on "Thorney Abbey," by the Rev. R. H. Warner (1879) has added to the further knowledge of this settlement.

At Whittlesea, near Peterborough, there is said to have been a congregation, but the authority is doubtful. At Stamford, the great Lord Burleigh took interest in the refugees settled there.

That the work of draining and converting the flat lands of Eastern England to productive use would be carried out partly by the Dutch is not a surprise, as we find that they applied to

Lincolnshire the skill which had been expended on Holland. At Sandtoft Chapel a colony of Dutch and French was gathered, and though their services were at first interrupted by dissensions among the landowners in 1681, a church was formed and a minister appointed.

This did not last long. In the neighbourhood are still to be found families descended from those who fled from France in 1685.

The congregation at Thorpe-le-Soken, in Essex, founded in 1683, is connected with Bishop Compton, of London, who approved of a transfer of the French service from the parish church, and ultimately of the erection of a chapel for their own use, which was opened in 1688.

Jean Severin was the first minister, but soon left this place for Greenwich, and about 1740 the congregation was dispersed.

As illustrating the relations of the Church of England and the refugees, we may mention that this community, having been thought wanting in loyalty to James II., a declaration to the opposite effect was sent to the Bishop of London and the magistrates; this document, as giving the signatures of the foreign residents, is of historical interest and import.

The churches where the refugees worshipped have, with the exception of some few in London, entirely disappeared, and in the provinces scanty remains tell the tale of former days. The descendants of those who fled to this country for conscience sake have conformed more or less to the English church. There yet remains, exactly as of old, enshrined in the noblest of England's Minsters, Canterbury Cathedral, the French church in the crypt, dating from the reign of Edward VI., surviving the ages of persecution—a witness, as it were, of the widespread nationality of the reformed religion. In that ancient crypt, stamped with the architectural skill of Prior Ernulf, service is still performed on Sundays, and the old Huguenot hymn, once sung in the rocky fastnesses of the Cevennes, goes forth undisturbed in these fair cathedral precincts. Around the interior walls, are French texts of Scripture; and tradition says that in these vaulted aisles the looms of the strangers were set up and worked.

The annals of this little church, which claims

its recognition from the hands of Edward VI. and Queen Elizabeth, and the only one now remaining in the county of Kent, may fitly close this chapter.

The first congregation was formed by the Walloons, or French-speaking Flemings, in 1550; it was then increased by the arrival of the Huguenots after St. Bartholomew (1572).

In time, the whole of the crypt was given up to the foreigners, their schools and meetings. Archbishop Cranmer and Parker showed much interest in the cause, and encouraged their services. In 1573 the religious freedom of the strangers was further approved by Royal Letters Patent, and Queen Elizabeth always supported their efforts. In 1574 the civil magistrates confirmed these privileges, and with the growing industries of the city, the refugees prospered in every way. In the visits to Canterbury of some of the Primates, this crypt church generally received their attention. In 1640, writes Somner, the Kentish historian, "The congregation, for the most part of distressed exiles, has grown so great and yet daily multiplying, that the place in short time is likely to prove a hive too little to contain such a swarm."

Some dark clouds now overshadowed our history, for Archbishop Laud, with this, as similar foreign congregations in his diocese, enforced the English liturgy and church government. The ministers of the crypt and other Protestant churches appealed to the Primate, but the matter was interrupted by the outbreak of the Civil War. Apart from that, internal dissensions arose, and in sketching the history of this community, it is impossible not to draw both its light and shade in order to a more perfect picture.

Secession on doctrinal grounds occasioned a severance of their place of worship, the new section adhering to the "Conformist or Anglican rite," and meeting in a part of the Archbishop's Palace near the cathedral. This disturbed state of affairs was referred to the principal church in London, and after a few years the congregations reunited in the crypt.

In 1662 Charles II., by an Order in Council, enjoined unity of worship both with the Walloons and the French, and for some fifty years the services were well maintained and harmonious.

In 1677 we read that there were 2800 Walloons and French in the city, and that their church was full to overflowing. The Revocation of the Edict of Nantes was at hand, and that event alone increased the foreign settlers, and for nearly a hundred years after 1685 a bright page of history opens on us. That period is much identified with the names of Archbishops Tenison, Wake, Herring, and Secker, all of whom took great interest not only in the ecclesiastical, but in the temporal welfare of the refugees. In the differences which arose, and which were referred to the Consistory in London, and at times to the ultimatum of the Archbishop, these Primates exercised a wise and liberal judgment.

An instance of this variance relates to the Walloons, who at times were made to contribute more than their just share in the maintenance of these services, receiving no part in the Royal Bounty fund of William and Mary. In their appeal for redress, the firm and generous support of Archbishop Tenison was given them. It would be impossible not to mention that Socinianism was a great element of discord among the refugees, and that a separate congregation adopting these tenets was founded, and called the "French Uniform church."

Their members, however, soon decreased, and many of them rejoined the " crypt " or attended some of the parish churches. The industries of Canterbury—silk-weaving, and other trades—contributed to the welfare of the foreign population, but when the manufactures fell off, a decline in the religious services followed.

This crisis arrived about the year 1790, when Spitalfields and Bethnal Green diverted the trade of Canterbury and left it at a low ebb, so much so that the minister and elders of the crypt church appealed to Archbishop Manners-Sutton for a portion of the Bounty Fund in support of their worship.

The Primate did not delay in the response; the then minister, François Durand, died, and his successor adopted the Prayer Book, translated into French. Thus, in a measure, the historical continuity of this service was broken by one diverse from the ancient Huguenot forms. Assistance was obtained to carry on the service, but that help was dependent on the use of the new liturgy.

From the years 1840 to 1870 the ministers of the French church in St. Martins-le-Grand officiated here till the Rev. J. A. Martin, B.D., the present able pastor,[3] was then appointed.

An appeal for the repair and improvement of this church has not been without result; the completion is still urged. "This congregation," writes the Rev. J. A. Martin, "is one of the monuments of that glorious but short reign of Edward VI., which was stamped with so many noble Christian deeds."

In 1875 the late Archbishop Tait warmly advocated its claims in the House of Lords. "While he granted that the number of persons attending the service was now very small, yet it was an institution which kept up a connection between the French Protestant Church and the Church of England, and therefore it appears very undesirable that the services should be unnecessarily interfered with."

Thus, after more than 300 years of existence, this little community has survived the changes of time, the ages of persecution, and the conflict of opinion, allied as it is to that noble cathedral, all the more noble because of its

---

[3] "Christian firmness of the Huguenots." By the Rev. J. A. Martin, B.D. 1881.

massive light and shade, the old and the new blending into one harmonious whole.

It is impossible not to include *some* of the refugees who became famous in the *rôle* of the cathedral, or were associated with the crypt or other of the Canterbury churches. Among the most prominent were Isaac Casaubon, Pierre du Moulin, and J. M. de l'Angle, whose lives have been alluded to in Chapter IV.

Du Moulin's name is already well known to students of Protestant history elsewhere than in England, and his connection with the Huguenot temple at Charenton, near Paris, is a memorable fact.

The De l'Angle family often appears in Kentish annals, as rector of St. George's, Canterbury, at Walmer, and Chartham, and other places.

We can only mention a few of the representative refugees who were allied with the English church in this district, such as Dampier, D'Ombrain, Durel, Castillion, Carrier, Herault, &c.

Among the crypt church ministers may be named some who have gained more than ordinary repute. These were Philippe le Keux, Pierre Trouillard, Jean Charpentier, François

Durand from Alençon, and Monsieur Janson. M. Trouillard was unfortunately pastor during the time when Socinianism reigned. The father of M. Charpentier was a martyr to the cruelty of Louis XIV., the son being at Canterbury; while the name of Durand was honourably known in this and the London refugee churches.

Charles le Cene, the eminent refugee, who put forth a new and noted version of the French Bible, cannot pass unnoticed. Born at Caen in 1647, he died in London in 1703, having once resided at Canterbury, where he is said to have officiated at the French Church there.

Among the inscriptions on tablet or tombstone, lingers many an historical name from France, and the districts of St. Alphage, Holy Cross, and St. Mildred are especially rich in such valuable memoranda.

In these parishes were the families of Baudry, Cordeaux, De Caufour, Delamotte, De Lassaux, Fedarb, Gambier, Le Grand, Lepine Miette, Pasquet, Ridout, Rondeau, Vellier, and others. This category would alone endorse, if not for other reasons, the language of Canon Jenkins, who, in his " Diocesan History of Canterbury," remarks, " The cathedral city has been for generations distinguished by an evangelical tone of preaching and sentiment which was the natural result of the vigorous element of foreign Protestantism early engrafted upon the native stock."

There is, however, something in the aspect of this ancient City which seems to open up, as it were, the whole story of Christianity from its introduction, to the vast assembly of American Prelates gathered in 1878 within its glorious cathedral. In that long interval, historical and stormy scenes have swept over it, superstition has happily been supplanted by truth, the Old and the New World meet in the teaching and lessons of its faith, so that the words of the late Dean Stanley, in his loving and learned researches into the "Memorials of Canterbury" appear to live again :—

" From Canterbury, the first English Christian city—from Kent, the first English Christian kingdom—has, by degrees arisen the whole constitution of Church and State in England, which now binds together the whole British Empire."

CHAPTER VI.

"Antiquity, after a time, has the grace of novelty."
                                                HAZLITT.

Refugee documents and archives—Registers of their churches—Somerset House, Record Office, and other libraries—The State Papers—Private and provincial collections—Inscriptions—Archives in Ireland—Printed books—Correspondence—Official and private—The "Savile Letters" and Lord Halifax—Publications of learned societies—Acts of the Synods—Study of the past.

AN important feature in the annals of any one community is the documentary aid we can obtain towards its history and progress.

This aid is to be found in the records, manuscripts, and printed literature, which, as regards refugee life in England, are very fully set forth in our public and private collections. We may place first the registers of the numerous French churches once in London. These records are now preserved at Somerset House, with others of the provincial chapels.

Such documents give, as it were, the key-note to history, by affording great genealogical data; they range from 1599 to about 1790, some few entries reaching to the year 1823. Besides ordinary contents, the registers often mention the names of the ministers of the several churches, occasionally the " Actes du Consistoire," with other matters. Some of the registers of the smaller congregations were kept, in early times, at the Threadneedle Street church, as the chief centre, till all were finally removed to Somerset House, as above mentioned.

Apart from these (so to speak) ecclesiastical archives, the constant intercourse of England with France led to several political despatches. Many of these relate to our subject, and all may be found arranged and edited in the series of "State Papers" so ably published under the auspices of the Public Record Office. From the reign of Elizabeth to Charles II., these papers teem with interest, and bring out many an incident of refugee life with the sympathy shown in England.

Another source are the MSS. in *private*

collections; of special reference to the foreign Protestants, are papers possessed by noblemen and gentlemen, those in the keeping of Lord Salisbury and the Marquis of Bath, at Longleat, being most important.

These documents have been made better known by the valuable reports of the Historical MSS. Commission, in which an abstract of their contents is given.

The subjects are various; some are letters of the exiled ministers, petitions, objections to restrictions, correspondence between Church dignitaries, noblemen and others, for the relief of the distressed and poorer refugees.

The manuscripts at our public institutions, at the British Museum, the University and college Libraries of Oxford and Cambridge, also claim attention. At Cambridge, are preserved the Vaudois papers, collected by Sir Samuel Morland, Cromwell's envoy in the Savoy, during that dire persecution; as a collateral subject with Huguenot history, these are of great interest. At Oxford, Archbishop Wake's collection, known as the "Christ Church letters," is of moment; that Primate's encouragement of the Protestants has already been noticed. This correspondence with the noted men of the day forms no unworthy parallel to a similar series in Lambeth Palace Library.

The records of the Dutch Church, Austin Friars,[1] preserved in the Guildhall, cannot be overlooked, nor those relating to the French refugees, in the same place. At Sion College, on the Embankment, will be found information as to foreign clergymen in London.

Not only London, but the provinces afford material for our subject, and naturally those towns where the exiles settled, give the best clue to their documentary annals.

Such are Bristol, Canterbury, Dover, Norwich, Plymouth, Rye, and other places; the gleanings from these spots being mostly found in the corporation records of each town, that of Canterbury being abundant in many ways.

In those city archives may be traced, in the admission of freemen, many a "stranger," whose occupation is sometimes described; much interest is derived from the perusal of the lists of the societies, or ancient guilds, as the Weavers', Dyers', Glass-makers', and others, who had their several charters of incorporation;

---

[1] "Registers of the Dutch Church." Edited by W. J. C. Moens. 1884.

in this way a forgotten link of family history can be supplied.

This brings me to the subject of parish registers as affording great assistance.

In the later years of refugee settlements, we find that many of the "strangers" attended our English churches, consequently their registers are, at times, very helpful in research.

This is particularly the case in the parishes of Holy Cross[2] and St. Alphage, Canterbury, whose registers are full of allusions to the parentage and condition of the inhabitants of those districts, who were chiefly weavers.

An instance of a cathedral register abounding in foreign genealogical data is Canterbury, which has been "edited" for the Harleian Society by Mr. R. Hovenden in 1878. It is urged that every such typical document should be thus made known; some Societies have done good work in printing the registers of the London churches; but in publishing one of the foreign congregations much might be accomplished, and the connection of the English with the refugees further established. While parish

---

[2] "Our Parish Books and what they tell us." By J. M. Cowper. 1884-5.

registers are usually kept in the churches to which they belong, we occasionally find them in private hands; an instance of this occurring in the Somerset House chapel-register, which was once in the possession of the late Sir Thomas Phillipps, of Cheltenham. As to the particular contents of these volumes, it is stated by Mr. J. S. Burn that "the register of the French church at Southampton is a model of careful guardianship; besides containing the usual births, deaths, and marriages, it refers to fasts, thanksgivings, and church affairs, with the list of the ministers." Further aid is to be had in the subscriptions collected in the different archdeaconries, which are often preserved with cathedral documents, or occasionally at the Record Office, London.

Assistance can also be found by consulting the minute books of the Consistories, and members' books, containing the names of those who came to the sacrament. In the churches, lists were often hung up of past ministers, elders, and deacons.

Besides ecclesiastical archives,[3] the collection of wills proved in each Diocese is of great importance to the historical student, and indeed

---

[3] Those at Fulham Palace, refer to refugee church history.

there is hardly a document which may not prove a mine of wealth.

The journals of the House of Lords, wherein many petitions and addresses are preserved of those seeking relief from our Government, give valuable particulars.

In a romantic, though not impossible way, much light could be thrown on the numbers and names of those who fled from France, by the returns said to be made by captains of vessels plying from that country to England.

History can also be written on stone; some of the most defined helps are the inscriptions and tablets in our cathedrals, churches, and churchyards. Here, again, refugee names occur, especially at Canterbury,[4] and we plead that all such fast-fading memorials, should be copied ere they become illegible.

> " An antique stone,
> The relics spared by old decay,
> As records often stand alone
> Of races that have passed away.
> And when historic light is thrown,
> With a dim uncertain ray,
> Traditions of an ancient state
> A ruin may corroborate."

---

[4] In the cathedral, its cloisters, and the city churches, several eminent foreign names are extant.

Art also steps in to the aid of history; the brush of Sir J. E. Millais and P. H. Calderon, R.A., has touchingly pourtrayed the noted scenes and sufferings of Huguenot life. Nor can prints or book illustrations or medals be ignored, as a great assistance to the subject.

To Ireland we turn with distinct knowledge that in her chief towns are preserved many records of a people to whom she showed kindly and welcome aid. At Dublin, existed a most interesting bond of union—for the documents relating to the Protestants of La Rochelle were once deposited in St. Patrick's Library, till 1862, when they were reclaimed by the Consistory of Rochelle, where they now remain.

The Corporation Records of Cork, Waterford, Youghal, and other cities, allude to the naturalization of the refugees, and that all who had fled their country on account of their religion be admitted free of the Corporation, with other encouragements for them to settle. In Ulster are to be found documents of interest, several of which have been printed in the Ulster *Journal of Archæology*. Besides the rich storehouse of manuscript lore, of which only the most typical examples have been cited, there is the wide field

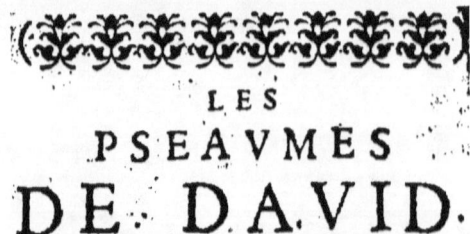

Facsimile of page from Psalm Book published at Nyort, 1670.

To face page 145.

of printed literature abounding in scope and variety.

The beginning of its career centres, as it were, round the reign of Edward VI., when the orders sanctioned by that King took visible form in type. Of this, John à Lasco's important treatise, entitled "La Discipline ecclésiastique des Églises reformées de France," printed in 1548, holds a leading place. We next notice the translations of the Scriptures, of the Psalms in rhyme by Beza and Clement Marot,[5] and of the many narratives of the persecutions, to which are sometimes added the historically interesting fact of their having been printed *Au désert*, referring possibly to the need of greater caution as to their place of imprint.

While such works were on the increase, permission was given by Edward VI. for a French Protestant in 1552 to set up a printing-press in England, also for the French king's licence to print the Bible in Paris. In the following year, 1553, the translation of our Prayer-Book into French was made by one Françoys Philippe, and

[5] The Psalms, set to music, early formed a part of family worship, or were sung in the streets and fields, and at large meetings by the assembled crowds.

this has been more fully described in Chapter I. p. 12.

Many publications now followed; some even give the lists[6] of those who suffered for conscience' sake. Through the dark days of Queen Mary few books appeared; but in the reign of Elizabeth, a brighter prospect opens, and the influx of the strangers after "St. Bartholomew" (1572) naturally brought its attendant train of published writings.

The cordiality of Archbishops Parker and Grindal to the exiles is an acknowledged fact, and many an episode of kindly help can be traced in the correspondence of these Prelates with learned divines in the volumes of the "Parker Society." During the seventeenth and eighteenth centuries periodical literature became very profuse, and its pages offered a welcome medium for the circulation of opinions. The pamphlet often assumed the guise of a letter addressed from the representatives of one State to another, wherein several matters would be discussed, as doctrinal differences, administration of relief, committees for help. In

---

[6] "Histoire ecclésiastique des Églises reformées de France." Anvers, 1580.

most of these cases the names of those who escaped from France appear, the lists being divided into those of position, the " bourgeoise," with others of reduced means. After the Revocation of the Edict of Nantes, writings of all kinds became more abundant, and we meet with letters of denization and naturalization, and in these, many important particulars occur.

The records of patents taken out for manufacturers, and reports of committees, give ample sources of information. An example of the latter occurs in a report of committee against a contraband trade which the French Protestants in London carried on with those abroad in 1698.

The correspondence between England and France before and after the above date, is strikingly instanced in what is known as the "Savile Letters," from Sir H. Savile, Envoy at Paris, and Vice-Chamberlain to Charles II. and James II., published by the Camden Society in 1858.

Savile's wish was to mitigate the severity of Louis XIV.'s dealings with the Protestants, and his colleague in England (Lord Halifax) was anxious to promote the same views, and thus writes :—

"I shall endeavour to justify my Protestantship by doing all that is in my power to the encouraging those that take sanctuary here out of France."

Again, Lord Halifax says (1679-80), "My credit with the French Protestants I owe wholly to you, your zeal being so notorious that it throweth a lustre upon all your poor relations."

Charenton was the headquarters of Protestantism, and this place seems to have attracted Sir H. Savile, who writes, in 1679, to Lord Halifax:—

"Having never failed Charenton one Sunday since I came into France, how much more this is for the King's service you cannot imagine, unless you saw how kindly these poor people take so small a countenancing as mine is."

In return, Lord Halifax writes:—"I approve of your going to Charenton, and your countenancing the Protestants, which I think the principal work of an English minister in France, but I am apt to believe it may make the Court there grow weary of you."

Six more years and the "Temple" at Charenton was levelled to the ground, while other Protestant churches were no more, for the "Edict" had gone forth!

Correspondence and despatches of the

nobility, bishops, divines, and others, crowd the periodical and official publications of the time, and we owe much to the learned societies who have printed the most important of these documents.

In this category may be named the Camden Society, in an article entitled "Foreigners resident in England, 1618—1688;" the Sussex Archæological in another, called, "Refugees in Sussex;" while the East Anglian settlements have found place in the Norfolk Antiquarian Miscellany. Several instances might be quoted by which obscure information has been brought to light and local topography enriched. In the by-ways, as it were, of history, many a hidden fact is revealed, and even the ordinary handbook is not to be overlooked.

Periodical literature held a long sway in refugee annals. It may be that the frequent anonymous style of the writing guaranteed safety in those inquisitorial times, and so preserved the continuity of the series.

The publication of the various "Acts of the Synods," those held at Charenton being specially famous, cannot be unnoticed. Several of these Acts were afterwards printed at Oxford.

As bearing on this subject, there is a MS. belonging to L. Majendie, Esq., which claims particular mention, as it is a "Mémoire de tous les Synodes nationaux." In the same possession, is the original manuscript of John à Lasco's "Discipline des Églises reformées," which has been before alluded to, and forms the key-note of the earlier annals of the foreign Protestant churches.

The varying information to be gleaned from MSS., books, prints, &c., is endless, and the intelligent study of them leads to the correction of much which has been conjectured, and to the increase of fresh truth. We live in an age when the clearer insight of every subject is acquired by investigation and help from the past; from the archives in our country, and the stores of printed literature, much may be gained. The late Dean Stanley said,[7] "Now, however, the time is come when a spirit prevails of juster appreciation of the past. It has grown up at the very moment when but for it every relic of antiquity would have disappeared.

"The bane and the antidote have grown side by side; and in this way we may be able to hand down to future generations the gifts and inheritances we have received from generations of old."

---

[7] Address—"Kent Archæological Society," 1858.

CHAPTER VII.

Present state of French Protestantism—Influence of the English Church abroad—The Coligny Monument—Dr. Bersier and churches in Paris—Foreign societies and their work—America and her co-operation—Churches still remaining—French Protestant Hospital—Archbishop Tait and his influence—Huguenot Society of London—Publications on refugee history—Bi-centenary of the "Revocation of the Edict of Nantes"—Conclusion.

THE later history of refugee life in England is a harder task to chronicle than its earlier career, as time and circumstances have blended it so intimately with our own surroundings. We cannot, however, dissociate the fact from the efforts made in France during the last fifty years for the increase of Protestantism, and its relations and influences with our own country. Many causes have aided this growth; several illustrious divines, politicians, and writers have combined not a little to advance these movements, and of such may be named—D'Aubigné,

Monod, Vinet, De Préssensé, Grandpierre, Thiers, Guizot, and others.

The building of churches in Paris, its neighbourhood, and the provinces has been one of the means of success, and in this, England has gladly shared in promoting their erection. Here may be specially instanced, the "Église de l'Étoile," which, finished soon after the Franco-German war (1870-1), takes a leading place in the annals of Paris. Its pastor, the Rev. Eugène Bersier, D.D., from having adapted a partly liturgical form to that already existing, has created a life and interest in the service of an inspiring character.

A movement to perpetuate the memory of a noble man, Admiral Coligny, has lately been set on foot, by proposing a monument near the very spot on which he fell in the fatal St. Bartholomew. The feeling England evinced, and the aid she afforded by subscription, cannot pass unnoticed, nor the fact that the Admiral's brother (Odet de Coligny) rests in our grandest minster, Canterbury Cathedral.

In Paris other means have been employed for the spread of Protestantism, and among them we may mention some of the societies, both religious and secular. The " Société de l'Histoire du Protestantisme Français," founded in 1852, occupies a most important and honourable position. By publishing proceedings[1] and by holding meetings in cities which have been the stronghold of the refugees, this society has done effective and scholarly work, and is supported by writers of known ability and position in France.

The conference at Nismes in 1883 was especially notable; the visits and services, of an historical character, commemorated the Protestantism of that ancient city, and the memory of those who suffered long in the Tour de Constance rather than deny their faith, was recalled, even through the lapse of many years. Assemblies of different religious societies at Berlin, Basle, Geneva, Paris, and elsewhere have had their successful results, and of these may be named the Evangelical Alliance, which has promoted many excellent schemes.

Another element marks the history and progress of Protestantism, viz. the synods held from

---

[1] "Bulletin historique et littéraire." Paris: Fischbacher, Rue de Seine, 33. London: Nutt, 270, Strand.

1559, and in particular that of 1872 in Paris, which discussed and formulated several important issues for the Reformed church of France.

Speaking of the present growing organization of the churches, the report (1884) of the Continental Society says: "This is indicative not only of the interest taken by the Church of Christ in these lands, but also of an increased responsibility on the part of French Protestants. The lethargy and timidity of the past are being abandoned, and the truly spiritual section of the Reformed Church are entering heartily into the work of evangelization."

It cannot but have been seen that in the earlier history of the refugees, America has stretched forth the hand of friendship to aid and guide, and that the vast emigration there some years ago, with the formation of French colonies, would naturally produce many bonds of union between the two countries.

This feeling will also be shared between England and the New World, or as so gracefully expressed by the late Dean Stanley's own words at New York (1878): "Of that unbroken union there seemed to me a likeness when, on the beautiful shores of Lake George, the Loch Katrine of America, I saw a maple and an oak-tree growing together from the same stem, perhaps from the same root—the brilliant, fiery maple, the emblem of America ; the gnarled and twisted oak, the emblem of England. So may the two nations always rise together, so different from each other, yet each springing from the same ancestral root."

To connect the various links of genealogy, Church history, and other matters, which crowd around the refugee annals of that continent, is one of the objects for which the " Huguenot Society of America " was founded in 1883.[2]

Dr. Storrs in his address in 1875 "On the early American spirit" says, "Whenever the history of those who came hither from La Rochelle and the banks of the Garonne is fully written, the value and vigour of the force which they imparted to the early American public life will need no demonstration."

As the learned chroniclers, so to speak, of French Protestant life in America, we cannot omit mention of the works, both published and to appear, of the Rev. Charles W. Baird, D.D.,

[2] See Appendix.

and of his brother, Professor Henry M. Baird, both of whom have an acknowledged high repute for the historical devotion and accuracy of their writings.

The words of Professor Baird at the inauguration of its Huguenot Society of America[3] may best describe the past and future of the emigration : " France herself did not lose them all, though long compelled to hide themselves, for now again, in our own days, the descendants of Huguenots are beginning to reassert their claim to a land, theirs by right of ancestral sacrifices and sufferings.

" Meanwhile, other countries, and America among the rest, have gained what France too freely and thoughtlessly parted with—a noble, heroic, Christian race."

Returning to England, we can now better trace the effects which have resulted from the once vast settlement in London, in the few remaining churches there devoted to the descendants of the refugees.

The churches so left have been already mentioned, viz., that of St. Martin's-le-Grand, St. Jean-en-Savoy in Bloomsbury Street, to which

[3] See Appendix.

may be added the comparatively recent building in Bayswater. All these are continuing the objects and work for which they were founded, and have attached to them, charitable and good societies. To that in Bloomsbury Street is annexed an excellent school, " L'École de Charité Protestante Française," founded in 1747, for the education and maintenance of young girls. The Bayswater church has many benevolent agencies, which have been successfully advanced by the minister, the Rev. Pontet-de-la-Harpe, B.D.

Another link with past history is the French Protestant Hospital, founded by Monsieur de Gastigny, and first situate in Bath Street, St. Luke's.

On the 12th of November, 1718, the chapel and buildings were opened and dedicated, the service being conducted by the Rev. Philippe Ménard, minister of the French Chapel, St. James'. The name of " La Providence " first given to this institution justly pourtrays its benevolent aims, while the Corporate seal, representing " Elijah fed by the ravens," carries out the same idea. Here the poorer refugees found a welcome home, after the sufferings and risks resulting from the Revocation of the Edict of Nantes.

The Hospice, originally founded in the parish of St. Luke's, was, in 1866, removed to Victoria Park, where, in a most picturesque building, erected from the designs of the late R. L. Roumieu, Esq., are accommodated sixty inmates, men and women, being poor descendants of the French Protestant refugees. Here in comfort, certainly which contrasts with the hardships their ancestors endured, the recipients of this admirable charity pass their later days (often after a toilsome life) in comfort and thankfulness.

The directors, chosen from the descendants of French Protestant families, administer the affairs of the hospital, to which is attached a valuable and increasing collection of books, prints, and documents relating to past history, and which may be freely consulted on proper introduction.[4]

It is trusted that this important library will become the fountain-head of reference on all subjects connected with the foreign Protestant

[4] The Secretary is A. Giraud Browning, Esq., 3, Victoria Street, Westminster.

communities. We have seen that the efforts to support and maintain the historical sequence of refugee life have not been without success, and that its cause was much strengthened and graced by the words of the late Archbishop Tait, who, in his Diocesan Charge (1876), referring to the long existence of the French Church in the crypt of Canterbury, said :—

"I do not forget that in this cathedral, though in an obscure part of it, there still remains a memorial of those days when the Church of England, looked to as the mother of the Protestant churches of Europe, gave an asylum to our persecuted Protestant brethren who came from other lands.

"This memorial of the past may have become now little more than a sentiment, but it is a sentiment not to be thought lightly of, and I consider it certainly no small honour of my Episcopate to have received, in consequence of a few words which I was able to speak in the House of Lords on the subject of those French Protestants, the thanks, as Chief Pastor of the Church of England, of a large and intelligent body of some seventy pastors of the Reformed

Protestant Church of France; so that there is something to remind us of our connection with those who, in distant lands, maintain under great disadvantages the truths for which the Reformers were contented to die."

In our own country, has just been established the "Huguenot Society of London,"[5] having almost similar aims and objects as carried out by our American brethren.

The "editing" and printing of the registers of the dissolved French churches will be one of the principal objects, while local and family history will be collected, preserved, and published.

In this nineteenth century we cannot ignore the opinions and sayings of many eminent men, both at home and abroad, on the subject of Protestantism. Père Hyacinthe Loyson, speaking before descendants of the Huguenots, said,—

" Je parle devant les fils des Huguenots, et je n'ai pas besoin de m'en souvenir pour rendre à leurs pères l'hommage qu'ils méritent. Ils ont realisé l'une des formes les plus pures et les plus héroïques de la conscience française, et les persécutions dont ils ont été l'objet les ont environnés

[5] See Appendix.

de la splendeur des martyrs, en nous laissant à nous-mêmes l'opprobre des bourreaux."

The writings of historical students have greatly increased the interest and importance of refugee literature. The labours of Baron F. De Schickler, by tracing out all their settlements in different European countries, in his learned work, "Les Églises du Refuge," have added much knowledge to the subject. The Rev. David Agnew, in his "Protestant Exiles from France," has opened up many new researches in genealogy and history, while Dr. Smile's "Huguenots" has long become a household word. Nor can the standard work "La France Protestante," by MM. les Frères Haag, pass unnoticed, nor the writings and essays of Weiss, Felice, Henri Bordier, R. S. Poole, and others of recent date. In this Bicentenary year of the Revocation of the Edict of Nantes, old memories are awakened and new impulses created to strengthen and add fresh influences to the Protestantism of the past and the future.

In this city of London has been celebrated the 200th anniversary of the passing of this "Edict" (October 22) by suitable services or appropriate meetings; an opportunity like this historic revival may have much power in directing the course of events—both at home and abroad. One proposal emanating from the recent Commemoration was, that scholarships be founded at Montauban to prepare young men of Huguenot parentage for the ministry. We may even see the famous "Temple at Charenton," once the rallying-point of the Huguenots, again take its place, though in a different way, for the spread of religion. The simile of a modern writer seems appropriately to recur to our minds—as he says,—

"At Queyras, in the Dauphiny Alps, a young elm grew by the side of a Protestant temple.

"In the days of persecution the temple was burnt, and the tree shared its fate; the persecutors, as tradition says, were wont to point to its charred stump and say tauntingly, 'When that elm blossoms, Protestantism will revive.' Now those who climb the valley can see for themselves how truly this tree was an image of Protestantism; its root, always alive, has been penetrating deeper and deeper into the rock, until it has received strength enough to blossom again."

These memories of the past should indeed strengthen the future of the Protestant Church, and though the events and cruelties of St. Bartholomew and of the reign of Louis XIV. have been softened by the hand of Time, we cannot dwell on them when every influence is moving onwards.

We have traced in these pages the outline of refugee life in England, and have seen its rise, progress, and absorption into our own nation.

In all these stages, can have been discerned the agencies and influences which have at times discouraged, at another cheered, the path of the "strangers."

Their biographies, as a beacon-light in the mists of superstition and error, seem to clear the way to a better appreciation of those noble characteristics which have been brought out through their story of sorrow and suffering. "From the furnace of distress and peril," says Mr. Poole, in his "Huguenots of the Dispersion," "the bright, generous characteristic of the race came out with quickened exhilaration."

"The light heart of the Celt was in them, purified from its vices, frivolity, and love of change; but Calvin himself could not destroy its verve."

English Protestantism has had interwoven into it those features which have added to its more perfect character; while courage, patience, industry, and fear of God, the distinguishing watch-word of the exiles, can still act as the motive power of all workers for good.

INDEX.

ABBADIE, J., 82.
Abbot, Archbishop, supports Refugee cause, 37.
Agnew, Rev. D., 161.
A Lasco, John, 6, 7, 8, 9, 10, 12, 13, 18, 25, 74; works of, 10; "Discipline des Églises," 145, 150.
Albemarle, Lord, writes for release of galley-slaves, 68.
Alexander, Peter, 7, 11.
Allix, P., life of, 95.
America, emigration to, 43; and the Refugees, 154—156; Huguenot Society of, 156.
Anne, Queen, 61; her interest in the refugees, 61—63.
Ascham, Roger, 7, 17.

BAIRD, Rev. C. W., 155.
———, H. M., 155.
Bancroft, Archbishop, 36; the Church in the Channel Isles under, 37.
Barlow, Bishop, 50.
Barnstaple, church at, 122.
Bedford, Duke of; aid to refugees, 68, 126.
Bersier, Dr., 20, 30, 31, 152.

Beza, 15.
Bible, anecdote of the, 4.
Bonnet, Dr., 15.
Bristol, congregation at, 121.
Bucer, 7; at Cambridge, 8.
Bulteel, J., minister at Canterbury, 113.
Burleigh, Lord, 26, 33, 126.
Burnet, Bishop, 46, 62, 88.
Butheau, C., 79.

CALVIN, John, 15, 17; influence and letters of, 15; corresponds with Edward VI. and Cranmer, 16; on reformation of English Church, 16.
Cambridge, Bucer at, 8.
Camden Society, the, 149.
Canons ecclésiastiques, 118, 119.
Canterbury, congregations at, 8, 9; crypt church in cathedral, 33, 34, 128—135; supported by Archbishops Cranmer and Parker, 129; by Tenison, Wake, Herring, and Secker, 131; by Queen Elizabeth, 129; under Charles II., 130; variances with Walloon

church, 131; Socinianism in, 131; present condition, 133; famous ministers, 134, 135; Archbishop Tait's plea for,133.
Canterbury industries of, 64, 132; foreign families and names in, 134, 135, 141; cathedral archives, 141, 143.
Casaubon, Isaac, 95, 96, 134.
Castoll, John, 35.
Cavallier, Jean, 106.
―――――, Rudolf, 13.
Cecil, Sir W., 12, 13.
Cevennois, prayer of the, 72.
Channel Isles, refugee churches in, 37, 47, 115—120; governors of, 116, 117; Prayer-Book for, 116; Somerset, Duke of, 116; under Elizabeth and James I., 117, 118; Archbishop Abbot and his policy, 118; under the Commonwealth, 118; under James II., 119.
Charenton, Temple at, 40, 95, 148, 162.
Charles I. and the refugees, 39—42; his action with foreign powers, 40—42.
Charles II., his conduct towards the Protestants, 46—50; death of, 50.
Chelsea, church at, 106.
Chenevix, family of, 101.
Church in the Desert, 72.
Colet, Dean, 7.
Coligny, Admiral, 29; character of, 30, 31; monument to, 152.
Coligny, Odet de, 29, 30.
Colomiez, P., 97.
Commonwealth, its influence on refugee history, 43, 45, 118.
Compton, Bishop, 46, 57—60; Evelyn's opinion of, 59; his care for the refugees, 59; and church at Thorpe-le-Soken,127.

Conformist congregations, 89.
Contributions for relief, 58.
Court, Antoine, 67, 71.
Cousin, Jean, Grindal's opinion of, 26.
Covenanters, the Scotch, 99.
Cranmer, Archbishop, 6, 8, 10, 11, 12, 13, 14, 16, 17; hospitality to strangers, 7; his doctrine, 9; "Catechism," 9; deprivation, 18; promoted foreign churches, 75.
Cromwell, his influence with the refugees, 43—45.

DARTMOUTH, refugees at, 120.
De Beauvoir, family of, 66.
De Bostaquet, 99, 100, 122.
De l'Angle, Jean M., 77, 134.
De la Fontaine, 101.
De la Motte, C., 83.
Denization, letters of, 49.
D'Espagne, M., 84, 85.
Dibon, M. de, 4.
Dissensions in foreign churches, 26.
D'Ombrain, H. H., 98.
Dover, settlement and church at, 111; foreign names around, 112.
Drelincourt, P., 100.
Dublin, refugee documents at, 144.
Du Bourdieu, L. A., 58, 82.
Du Moulin, 77, 78, 134.
Durand, 79, 83.
Durel, Jean, 47, 48, 81, 82
Durham House, chapel in, 85.
Du Veil, C., 96.
Dutch Church, The, 140.

EAST Anglian settlements, 126.
Edward VI., 14; reign and death, 17, 18; words of Calvin to, 17.
Elizabeth, foreign policy of, 22;

Index.

Huguenot church under, 22; her reception of Coligny, 31; St. Bartholomew and the Queen, 32; safety of, 33; reception of, by Archbishop Parker, 34; government of Channel Isles, 116, 117.
Erasmus, 5, 6.
Etaples, 3.
Evelyn, John, at Greenwich, 103.
Exeter, petition of French Protestants at, 92; settlement and church at, 122; tapestry manufacture, 123.

FABER, family of, 3.
Farel, William, 3, 4.
Faversham, foreigners at, 114.
Fleury, family of, 99.
Foreigners in London, returns of, 25.
François, Richard, 11.
Frankfort, church at, 11, 18.
French Protestant Hospital, the, 157, 158.
Fuller, Dr. Thomas, 80.

GALLEY slaves, aid for, 69.
Galway, Lord, 57, 61.
Glastonbury, church at, 13; support of, by Somerset and Cranmer, 13, 14; service of, 14.
Geneva, 5, 17.
Greenwich, settlement at, 60, 61, 103, 104.
Gresham, Sir Thomas, his reception of Odet de Coligny, 29.
Grindal, Archbishop, 22—24; superintendent of foreign churches, 25; opinion of Jean Cousin, 26; dissensions in churches dealt with by, 26; aid to refugees, 34; and the Threadneedle Street church, 76.
Guernsey, *vide* Channel Isles.
Guilds, lists of, 141.

HAAG, M., 161.
Halifax, Lord, 148.
Hammersmith, settlement at, 106.
Herring, Archbishop, his care for the exiles, 68, 69; correspondence of, 68; interposed for release of galley slaves, 69; and Dr. Jortin, 98; Jersey exiles, 120; and Mr. Majendie, 90.
Horne, Bishop, 115.
Huguenot Society of London, the, 160; of America, 156.
Hythe, settlement at, 113, 114.

INSCRIPTIONS, refugee, 143.
Ireland, fugitives in, 98—102; archives and documents in, 144.

JAMES I. and the foreign Protestants, 36.
James II. and the refugees, 50, 51.
Jersey, *vide* Channel Isles.
———, Deans of, 119, 120.
Jewel, Bishop, 32.
Jortin, Dr., 5, 97, 98.

KENT, industries of, 110.

LA ROCHELLE, disaster of, 40.
Laud, Archbishop, his policy towards the Huguenots, 41, 42, 113.
Lausanne, college at, 67.
Lavington, Bishop of Exeter, 92.
Lefevre, Jacques, 3, 5.
Letters patent, 49, 59.
Lloyd, Bishop of Worcester, 60.

Lloyd, Bishop of St. Asaph, 83.
London, foreign congregations in, 7, 9, 22, 75, 76; first ministers, 10, 12, 77, 78; St. Austin's church, 9, 11; St. Anthony's hospital, 10, 74; Threadneedle Street church, 75; its ministers, 77, 78; Synods there, 76; Library, 77; Huguenot Society of, 159; Protestant sympathy of, 18.
Louis XIV., 44, 53.
Loyson, Père Hyacinthe, 160.

MAIDSTONE, Dutch and Flemings at, 114; St. Faith's Chapel, 114; foreign industries, 114.
Majendie, Mr., and Archbishop Secker, 90, 93, 122.
Marian persecutions, the, 19.
Martin, M., 79.
Martin's-le-Grand, St., French church at, 76, 156.
Martyr, Peter, 7, 9, 18.
Mercier, 79.
Minute books of consistories, 142.
More, Sir Thomas, 5.
Morland, Sir S , 44 ; and MSS. at Cambridge, 44.

NANTES, Revocation of Edict of, effects and results in England and France, 52—55; Bi-centenary Celebration in London, 161.
Naturalization Bill, 62.
Nismes, conference at, 153.
"Nod," Mount, cemetery at, and refugee names, 105.
Norwich, Walloons at, 27; dissensions of church at, 28; French refugees at, 28; exodus from, 42; episcopate of Bishop Jegon, 43; churches at, 123—126; ministers of, 125; "discipline" of, 123; religious differences, 125; foreign families at, 126.

OXFORD University and foreign Protestants, 44.

PALISSY, 3.
Pamphlets on relief fund, 92 ; on refugees, 146.
Paris, Protestant churches in, 152; Société du Protestantisme Français, 153.
Parish registers, 141.
Parker, Archbishop, 22—24; policy of, 26; and church at Norwich, 27 ; prayers for Elizabeth's safety, 33; reception of, at Canterbury, 34; care for French church there, 34; at Sandwich, 113.
Parker Society publications, 146.
Patents, records of, 147.
Paul's Cross, sermons at, 23.
Plymouth, foreign church at, 121, 122.
Poissy, conference at, 11, 15, 24.
Pollandus, V., 14.
Portarlington, church at, 100.
Prayer-Book in French, 12, 145; for Channel Isles, 116, 118.
Press, a French printing-, 12, 145.
Printed literature of refugees, 144.
Psalms, the, in metre, 145.
Puritanism, 15, 24.

RAPIN, T. de, 101.
Reformed Church, increase of, abroad, 154.
Refugee documents at public institutions, 139; at the Uni-

versities, 139; in London, 140; lists in London, 25.
Registers of foreign churches, 138.
Registers, publication of, 141.
Restoration, the, 45.
Ridley, Bishop of London, 10, 75.
Rivière, François de, 8, 62.
Romaine, W., 98.
Romilly, 79.
Royal Bounty Fund, 57, 70, 71, 89; its history, 90—94.
Royal Exchange, London, 29, 30.
Russell, Lady Rachel, 53, 61.
Ruvigny, Marquis, 57, 60, 61, 103, 104.
Rye, settlement and church at, 106—111; ministers at, 109; foreign names, 110; aspect of, 111.

SANCROFT, Archbishop, 57; care for refugees, 58.
Sandtoft chapel, 127.
Sandwich, church at, 113; visited by Archbishop Parker, 113; trades at, 113; during Laud's Primacy, 113.
Saurin, Louis, 78.
Savile letters, the, 147.
Savoy church, 47, 79; its history and ministers, 80—83; removed to Bloomsbury, 81, 156.
Schickler, Baron F. de, his works, 161.
Schomberg, 57, 82.
Scriptures, printing of, 2—4.
Secker, Archbishop, 70; his aid to the Genevan ministers, 70; to the Royal Bounty Fund, 70, 71; and Mr. Majendie, 90—94; continues Bounty Fund, 93; interest in Canterbury refugees, 131.

Severin, Jean, 127.
Sevigné, Madame de, 52, 82.
Sheldon, Bishop, 80, 81.
Smiles, Dr., 161.
Society for Foreign Protestants, 69; and Archbishop Herring, 69; in Ireland, 69.
Soho, churches in and around, 87, 88.
Somerset, Duke of, 12, 13, 14, 18, 116.
Somerset House, French service in, 84; registers at, 138.
Southampton, settlement and church at, 115.
Spitalfields, churches and history of, 86, 87.
Spital sermons, 87.
Stamford, refugees at, 126.
State papers, the, 138; records in public and private collections, 139.
St. Bartholomew massacre, the, 28, 29. 32, 33.
St. James's Palace, Chapel Royal, 88.
Stonehouse, refugees at, 121.
Sussex, refugees in, 110.
Synods held in London, 76; Acts of the, 149; history of, 154.

TAIT, Archbishop, on refugee Protestants, 133, 159.
Tenison, Archbishop, and the Weavers' Company, 64; and church at Rye, 109, 110; support of Canterbury church, 131; and Royal Bounty Fund, 131.
Thorney Abbey, 48, 126.
Thorpe-le-Soken, 127.
Threadneedle Street, French church, *vide* London.
Tillotson, Archbishop, 60.
Trelawney, Bishop, 119, 121.

Tremellius, 7, 13.
Trench, family of, 101.

ULSTER, settlements in, 99.
Uniformity, Act of, 48, 49, 118.
Union of Protestant churches, 16, 17, 45; with Gallican Church, 65.
Utenhovius, 8.

VAUDOIS, the, 43, 69.
Vauville, Richard, 11, 77.
Vignoles family, 100.

WAKE, Archbishop, 65; his efforts for union with Gallican Church, 65; MSS. at Oxford and Lambeth, 66; college at Lausanne, 67; his work, 67; aid to Canterbury refugees, 131.
Walloon church, the, 13, 75; differences between, and French, 48.
Wandsworth, refugees and church at, 104, 105.
Warham, Archbishop, 5, 6.
Waterford, church at, 99.
Whitgift, Archbishop, his encouragement of the exiles, 35.
Whittlesea, church at, 126.
William III., 56; character of, 57; his chapel at Kensington Palace, 90; Parliamentary relief for refugees, 59, 91.
Wills, diocesan, 142.
Winchelsea, 110.
Wren, Bishop of Norwich, 42.

APPENDIX.

HUGUENOT SOCIETY OF LONDON.

President—Right Hon. Sir H. Austen Layard, G.C.B.

This Society (founded April, 1885) has the following

OBJECTS.

(1.) The interchange and publication of knowledge relating to:—

    (A) The history of the Huguenots in France.
    (B) The Huguenot Emigrations from France and adjoining countries.
    (C) The Refugee Settlements throughout the world, particularly those in Great Britain, Ireland, and the Channel Islands; and the resulting effects of those Settlements upon the professions, manufactures, commerce, and social life of the several places in which they were made.
    (D) Huguenot genealogy and heraldry and Huguenot Church and other Registers.

(2.) To form a bond of fellowship among some of those who inherit or admire the characteristic Huguenot virtues, and who desire to perpetuate the memory of their Huguenot ancestors.

The Society will also undertake, under the direction of the Council, as opportunities arise and the funds of the Society permit, the publication of Huguenot Church Registers, genealogies, inedited documents, and other information bearing upon Huguenot history.

Publications of parts have been issued, and a forthcoming number will contain an account of the Bi-Centenary celebration in London, October, 1885.

The present Honorary Secretary is A. Giraud Browning, Esq., Honorary Secretary of the French Protestant Hospital, Victoria Park, E.

HUGUENOT SOCIETY OF AMERICA,

Founded in 1883, has issued a part of proceedings, has held memorial meetings both on the anniversary of the "St. Bartholomew" (24th August), and at the Revocation Bi-Centenary. The Hon. John Jay is Chairman of the Society, and its address is New York City.

BY THE SAME AUTHOR.

ART TREASURES

OF THE

LAMBETH LIBRARY.

A DESCRIPTION OF THE ILLUMINATED MSS., WITH NOTES ON THE LIBRARY. Price 14s,

PICKERING: London, 1873.

Opinions of the Press.

"All who love books will warmly thank Mr. Kershaw, Librarian at Lambeth Palace, for his compact volume. The details given are amply sufficient to direct the attention of those interested in illuminated MSS.; and nothing could be better than the outline specimens in lithography,"—*Standard.*

"We cordially commend the volume in general terms as precisely the style of work that may be a model for any and every description of art treasures."—*Art Journal.*

Notes on Croydon Palace; its History and Associations.
Croydon: F. Warren. 8vo. 1877.

"Mr. Kershaw has given a graphic sketch of the history and present condition of the palace in Croydon—the essay is well deserving attention."—*Architect.*

"We strongly recommend this pamphlet to those visiting the old palace."—*Morning Post.*

Famous Kentish Houses; their History and Architecture.
B. T. Batsford, 52, High Holborn. J. Burgess-Brown, Maidstone. *Illustrated.* 1880.

"Avoiding lengthy details, the author has conveyed in a pleasant manner a clear idea of the chief characteristics of the many castles and mansions for which this county is famous, and has thus added another contribution to Kentish archæology."—*Kentish Express.*

Foreign Refugee Settlements in East Kent.
(British Archæological Society Journal.) 1884.

A Catalogue of American and Foreign Books Published or Imported by Messrs. Sampson Low & Co. *can be had on application.*

Crown Buildings, 188, Fleet Street, London,
October, 1885.

A Selection from the List of Books

PUBLISHED BY

SAMPSON LOW, MARSTON, SEARLE, & RIVINGTON.

ALPHABETICAL LIST.

ABOUT Some Fellows. By an Eton Boy, Author of "A Day of my Life." Cloth limp, square 16mo, 2s. 6d.

Adams (C. K.) Manual of Historical Literature. Cr. 8vo, 12s. 6d.

Alcott (Louisa M.) Jack and Jill. 16mo, 5s.
—— *Old-Fashioned Thanksgiving Day.* 3s. 6d.
—— *Proverb Stories.* 16mo, 3s. 6d.
—— *Spinning-Wheel Stories.* 16mo, 5s.
—— See also "Rose Library."

Alden (W. L.) Adventures of Jimmy Brown, written by himself. Illustrated. Small crown 8vo, cloth, 2s. 6d.

Aldrich (T. B.) Friar Jerome's Beautiful Book, &c. Very choicely printed on hand-made paper, parchment cover, 3s. 6d.
—— *Poetical Works.* Edition de Luxe. 8vo, 21s.

Alford (Lady Marian) Needlework as Art. With over 100 Woodcuts, Photogravures, &c. Royal 8vo, 42s.; large paper, 84s.

Amateur Angler's Days in Dove Dale: Three Weeks' Holiday in July and August, 1884. By E. M. Printed by Whittingham, at the Chiswick Press. Cloth gilt, 1s. 6d.; fancy boards, 1s.

American Men of Letters. Thoreau, Irving, Webster. 2s. 6d. each.

Anderson (W.) Pictorial Arts of Japan. With 80 full-page and other Plates, 16 of them in Colours. Large imp. 4to, gilt binding, gilt edges, 8l. 8s.; or in four parts, 2l. 2s. each.

Angler's Strange Experiences (An). By Cotswold Isys. With numerous Illustrations, 4to, 5s. New Edition, 3s. 6d.

Angling. See Amateur, "British Fisheries Directory," "Cutcliffe," "Martin," "Stevens," "Theakston," "Walton," and "Wells."

Arnold (Edwin) Birthday Book. 4s. 6d.

A

Biographies of the Great Artists (continued) :—

Leonardo da Vinci.
Little Masters of Germany, by W. B. Scott.
Mantegna and Francia.
Meissonier, by J. W. Mollett, 2s. 6d.
Michelangelo Buonarotti, by Clément.
Murillo, by Ellen E. Minor, 2s. 6d.
Overbeck, by J. B. Atkinson.
Raphael, by N. D'Anvers.
Rembrandt, by J. W. Mollett.
Reynolds, by F. S. Pulling.
Rubens, by C. W. Kett.
Tintoretto, by W. R. Osler.
Titian, by R. F. Heath.
Turner, by Cosmo Monkhouse.
Vandyck and Hals, by P. R. Head.
Velasquez, by E. Stowe.
Vernet and Delaroche, by J. Rees.
Watteau, by J. W. Mollett, 2s. 6d.
Wilkie, by J. W. Mollett.

Bird (F. J.) American Practical Dyer's Companion. 8vo, 42s.

Bird (H. E.) Chess Practice. 8vo, 2s. 6d.

Black (Wm.) Novels. See "Low's Standard Library."

Blackburn (Charles F.) Hints on Catalogue Titles and Index
Entries, with a Vocabulary of Terms and Abbreviations, chiefly from Foreign Catalogues. Royal 8vo, 14s.

Blackburn (Henry) Breton Folk. With 171 Illust. by RANDOLPH
CALDECOTT. Imperial 8vo, gilt edges, 21s.; plainer binding, 10s. 6d.

—— *Pyrenees (The).* With 100 Illustrations by GUSTAVE
DORÉ, corrected to 1881. Crown 8vo, 7s. 6d.

Blackmore (R. D.) Lorna Doone. Edition de luxe. Crown 4to,
very numerous Illustrations, cloth, gilt edges, 31s. 6d.; parchment, uncut, top gilt, 35s. Cheap Edition, small post 8vo, 6s.

—— *Novels.* See "Low's Standard Library."

Blaikie (William) How to get Strong and how to Stay so.
Rational, Physical, Gymnastic, &c., Exercises. Illust., sm. post 8vo, 5s.

—— *Sound Bodies for our Boys and Girls.* 16mo, 2s. 6d.

Bonwick (Jos.) British Colonies and their Resources. 1 vol.,
cloth, 5s. Sewn—I. Asia, 1s.; II. Africa, 1s.; III. America, 1s.; IV. Australasia, 1s.

Bosanquet (Rev. C.) Blossoms from the King's Garden : Sermons
for Children. 2nd Edition, small post 8vo, cloth extra, 6s.

Boussenard (L.) Crusoes of Guiana. Illustrated. 5s.

—— *Gold-seekers, a Sequel.* Illustrated. 16mo, 5s.

Boy's Froissart. King Arthur. Mabinogion. Percy. See
LANIER.

Bradshaw (J.) New Zealand as it is. 8vo, 12s. 6d.

Brassey (Lady) Tahiti. With 31 Autotype Illustrations after
Photos. by Colonel STUART-WORTLEY. Fcap. 4to, 21s.

Bright (John) Public Letters. Crown 8vo, 7s. 6d.

Brisse (Baron) Ménus (366). A *ménu*, in French and English, for every Day in the Year. Translated by Mrs. MATTHEW CLARKE. 2nd Edition. Crown 8vo, 5s.
British Fisheries Directory, 1883-84. Small 8vo, 2s. 6d.
Brittany. See BLACKBURN.
Brown. Life and Letters of John Brown, Liberator of Kansas, and Martyr of Virginia. By F. B. SANBORN. Illustrated. 8vo, 12s. 6d.
Browne (G. Lennox) Voice Use and Stimulants. Sm. 8vo, 3s. 6d.
—— *and Behnke (Emil) Voice, Song, and Speech.* Illustrated, 3rd Edition, medium 8vo, 15s.
Bryant (W. C.) and Gay (S. H.) History of the United States. 4 vols., royal 8vo, profusely Illustrated, 60s.
Bryce (Rev. Professor) Manitoba. With Illustrations and Maps. Crown 8vo, 7s. 6d.
Bunyan's Pilgrim's Progress. With 138 original Woodcuts. Small post 8vo, cloth gilt, 3s. 6d.; gilt edges, 4s.
Burnaby (Capt.) On Horseback through Asia Minor. 2 vols., 8vo, 38s. Cheaper Edition, 1 vol., crown 8vo, 10s. 6d.
Burnaby (Mrs. F.) High Alps in Winter; or, Mountaineering in Search of Health. By Mrs. FRED BURNABY. With Portrait of the Authoress, Map, and other Illustrations. Handsome cloth, 14s.
Butler (W. F.) The Great Lone Land; an Account of the Red River Expedition, 1869-70. New Edition, cr. 8vo, cloth extra, 7s. 6d.
—— *Invasion of England, told twenty years after, by an Old* Soldier. Crown 8vo, 2s. 6d.
—— *Red Cloud; or, the Solitary Sioux.* Imperial 16mo, numerous illustrations, gilt edges, 5s.
—— *The Wild North Land; the Story of a Winter Journey* with Dogs across Northern North America. 8vo, 18s. Cr. 8vo, 7s. 6d.
Buxton (H. J. W.) Painting, English and American. Crown 8vo, 5s.

CADOGAN (Lady A.) Illustrated Games of Patience. Twenty-four Diagrams in Colours, with Text. Fcap. 4to, 12s. 6d.
California. See "Nordhoff."
Cambridge Staircase (A). By the Author of "A Day of my Life at Eton." Small crown 8vo, cloth, 2s. 6d.

Cambridge Trifles; from an Undergraduate Pen. By the Author of "A Day of my Life at Eton," &c. 16mo, cloth extra, 2s. 6d.

Carleton (Will) Farm Ballads, Farm Festivals, and Farm Legends. 1 vol., small post 8vo, 3s. 6d.

—— *City Ballads.* With Illustrations. 12s. 6d.

—— See also "Rose Library."

Carnegie (A.) American Four-in-Hand in Britain. Small 4to, Illustrated, 10s. 6d. Popular Edition, 1s.

—— *Round the World.* 8vo, 10s. 6d.

Chairman's Handbook (The). By R. F. D. PALGRAVE, Clerk of the Table of the House of Commons. 5th Edition, 2s.

Changed Cross (The), and other Religious Poems. 16mo, 2s. 6d.

Charities of London. See Low's.

Chattock (R. S.) Practical Notes on Etching. Sec. Ed., 8vo, 7s. 6d.

Chess. See BIRD (H. E.).

Children's Praises. Hymns for Sunday-Schools and Services. Compiled by LOUISA H. H. TRISTRAM. 4d.

Choice Editions of Choice Books. 2s. 6d. each. Illustrated by C. W. COPE, R.A., T. CRESWICK, R.A., E. DUNCAN, BIRKET FOSTER, J. C. HORSLEY, A.R.A., G. HICKS, R. REDGRAVE, R.A., C. STONEHOUSE, F. TAYLER, G. THOMAS, H. J. TOWNSHEND, E. H. WEHNERT, HARRISON WEIR, &c.

Bloomfield's Farmer's Boy.	Milton's L'Allegro.
Campbell's Pleasures of Hope.	Poetry of Nature. Harrison Weir.
Coleridge's Ancient Mariner.	Rogers' (Sam.) Pleasures of Memory.
Goldsmith's Deserted Village.	Shakespeare's Songs and Sonnets.
Goldsmith's Vicar of Wakefield.	Tennyson's May Queen.
Gray's Elegy in a Churchyard.	Elizabethan Poets.
Keat's Eve of St. Agnes.	Wordsworth's Pastoral Poems.

"Such works are a glorious beatification for a poet."—*Athenæum.*

Christ in Song. By PHILIP SCHAFF. New Ed., gilt edges, 6s.

Chromo-Lithography. See "Audsley."

Collingwood (Harry) Under the Meteor Flag. The Log of a Midshipman. Illustrated, small post 8vo, gilt, 6s.; plainer, 5s.

—— *The Voyage of the "Aurora."* Illustrated, small post 8vo, gilt, 6s.; plainer, 5s.

Colvile (H. E.) Accursed Land: Water Way of Edom. 10s. 6d.

Composers. See "Great Musicians."

Confessions of a Frivolous Girl. Cr. 8vo, 6s. Paper boards, 1s.

Cook (Dutton) Book of the Play. New Edition. 1 vol., 3s. 6d.

────── *On the Stage: Studies of Theatrical History and the Actor's Art.* 2 vols., 8vo, cloth, 24s.

Costume. See SMITH (J. MOYR).

Cowen (Jos., M.P.) Life and Speeches. By MAJOR JONES. 8vo, 14s.

Curtis (C. B.) Velazquez and Murillo. With Etchings, &c. Royal 8vo, 31s. 6d.; large paper, 63s.

Custer (E. B.) Boots and Saddles. Life in Dakota with General Custer. Crown 8vo, 8s. 6d.

Cutcliffe (H. C.) Trout Fishing in Rapid Streams. Cr. 8vo, 3s. 6d.

*D*ANVERS (N.) *An Elementary History of Art.* Crown 8vo, 10s. 6d.

────── *Elementary History of Music.* Crown 8vo, 2s. 6d.

────── *Handbooks of Elementary Art—Architecture; Sculpture; Old Masters; Modern Painting.* Crown 8vo, 3s. 6d. each.

Davis (C. T.) Manufacture of Bricks, Tiles, Terra-Cotta, &c. Illustrated. 8vo, 25s.

────── *Manufacture of Leather.* With many Illustrations. 52s. 6d.

Dawidowsky (F.) Glue, Gelatine, Isinglass, Cements, &c. 8vo, 12s. 6d.

Day of My Life (A); or, Every-Day Experiences at Eton. By an ETON BOY. 16mo, cloth extra, 2s. 6d.

Day's Collacon: an Encyclopædia of Prose Quotations. Imperial 8vo, cloth, 31s. 6d.

Decoration. Vols. II. to IX. New Series, folio, 7s. 6d. each.

Dogs in Disease: their Management and Treatment. By ASHMONT. Crown 8vo, 7s. 6d.

Donnelly (Ignatius) Atlantis; or, the Antediluvian World. 7th Edition, crown 8vo, 12s. 6d.

────── *Ragnarok: The Age of Fire and Gravel.* Illustrated, Crown 8vo, 12s. 6d.

Doré (Gustave) Life and Reminiscences. By BLANCHE ROOSE-
VELT. With numerous Illustrations from the Artist's previously un-
published Drawings. Medium 8vo, 24s.

Dougall (James Dalziel) Shooting: its Appliances, Practice,
and Purpose. New Edition, revised with additions. Crown 8vo, 7s. 6d.
"The book is admirable in every way. . . . . We wish it every success."—*Globe.*
"A very complete treatise. . . . Likely to take high rank as an authority on shooting."—*Daily News.*

Drama. See COOK (DUTTON).

Dyeing. See BIRD (F. J.).

EDUCATIONAL Works published in Great Britain. A
Classified Catalogue. Second Edition, 8vo, cloth extra, 5s.

Egypt. See "De Leon," "Foreign Countries."

Eight Months on the Gran Ciacco of the Argentine Republic.
8vo, 12s. 6d.

Electricity. See GORDON.

Elliot (Adm. Sir G.) Future Naval Battles, and how to Fight
them. Numerous Illustrations. Royal 8vo, 14s.

Emerson (R. W.) Life. By G. W. COOKE. Crown 8vo, 8s. 6d.

English Catalogue of Books. Vol. III., 1872—1880. Royal
8vo, half-morocco, 42s. See also "Index."

English Etchings. A Periodical published Monthly.

English Philosophers. Edited by E. B. IVAN MÜLLER, M.A.

A series intended to give a concise view of the works and lives of English
thinkers. Crown 8vo volumes of 180 or 200 pp., price 3s. 6d. each.

Francis Bacon, by Thomas Fowler.	*John Stuart Mill, by Miss Helen Taylor.
Hamilton, by W. H. S. Monck.	Shaftesbury and Hutcheson, by Professor Fowler.
Hartley and James Mill, by G. S. Bower.	Adam Smith, by J. A. Farrer.

* *Not yet published.*

Esmarch (Dr. Friedrich) Treatment of the Wounded in War.
Numerous Coloured Plates and Illust., 8vo, strongly bound, 1l. 8s.

Etching. See CHATTOCK, and ENGLISH ETCHINGS.

Etchings (Modern) of Celebrated Paintings. 4to, 31s. 6d.

FARM Ballads, Festivals, and Legends. See "Rose Library."

Fauriel (Claude) Last Days of the Consulate. Cr. 8vo, 10s. 6d.

Fawcett (Edgar) A Gentleman of Leisure. 1s.

Feilden (H. St. C.) Some Public Schools, their Cost and Scholarships. Crown 8vo, 2s. 6d.

Fenn (G. Manville) Off to the Wilds: A Story for Boys. Profusely Illustrated. Crown 8vo, 7s. 6d. ; also 5s.

—— *The Silver Cañon: a Tale of the Western Plains.* Illustrated, small post 8vo, gilt, 6s.; plainer, 5s.

Fennell (Greville) Book of the Roach. New Edition, 12mo, 2s.

Ferns. See HEATH.

Fields (J. T.) Yesterdays with Authors. New Ed., 8vo, 10s. 6d.

Fleming (Sandford) England and Canada: a Summer Tour. Crown 8vo, 6s.

Florence. See "Yriarte."

Folkard (R., Jun.) Plant Lore, Legends, and Lyrics. Illustrated, 8vo, 16s.

Forbes (H. O.) Naturalist's Wanderings in the Eastern Archipelago. Illustrated, 8vo, 21s.

Foreign Countries and British Colonies. A series of Descriptive Handbooks. Crown 8vo, 3s. 6d. each.

Australia, by J. F. Vesey Fitzgerald.
Austria, by D. Kay, F.R.G.S.
*Canada, by W. Fraser Rae.
Denmark and Iceland, by E. C. Otté.
Egypt, by S. Lane Poole, B.A.
France, by Miss M. Roberts.
Germany, by S. Baring-Gould.
Greece, by L. Sergeant, B.A.
*Holland, by R. L. Poole.
Japan, by S. Mossman.
*New Zealand.
*Persia, by Major-Gen. Sir F. Goldsmid.
Peru, by Clements R. Markham, C.B.
Russia, by W. R. Morfill, M.A.
Spain, by Rev. Wentworth Webster.
Sweden and Norway, by F. H. Woods.
*Switzerland, by W. A. P. Coolidge, M.A.
*Turkey-in-Asia, by J. C. McCoan, M.P.
West Indies, by C. H. Eden, F.R.G.S.

* *Not ready yet.*

Frampton (Mary) Journal, Letters, and Anecdotes, 1799—1846. 8vo, 14s.

Franc (Maud Jeanne). The following form one Series, small post 8vo, in uniform cloth bindings, with gilt edges :—

Emily's Choice. 5s.	Vermont Vale. 5s.
Hall's Vineyard. 4s.	Minnie's Mission. 4s.
John's Wife: A Story of Life in South Australia. 4s.	Little Mercy. 4s.
	Beatrice Melton's Discipline. 4s.
Marian; or, The Light of Some One's Home. 5s.	No Longer a Child. 4s.
	Golden Gifts. 4s.
Silken Cords and Iron Fetters. 4s.	Two Sides to Every Question. 4s.
Into the Light. 4s.	Master of Ralston, 4s.

Francis (Frances) Elric and Ethel: a Fairy Tale. Illustrated. Crown 8vo, 3s. 6d.

French. See "Julien."

Froissart See "Lanier

Gale (F.; the Old Buffer) Modern English Sports: their Use and Abuse. Crown 8vo, 6s.; a few large paper copies, 10s. 6d.

Garth (Philip) Ballads and Poems from the Pacific. Small post 8vo, 6s.

Gentle Life (Queen Edition). 2 vols. in 1, small 4to, 6s.

THE GENTLE LIFE SERIES.

Price 6s. each; or in calf extra, price 10s. 6d.; Smaller Edition, cloth extra, 2s. 6d., except where price is named.

The Gentle Life. Essays in aid of the Formation of Character of Gentlemen and Gentlewomen.

About in the World. Essays by Author of "The Gentle Life."

Like unto Christ. A New Translation of Thomas à Kempis' "De Imitatione Christi."

Familiar Words. An Index Verborum, or Quotation Handbook. 6s.

Essays by Montaigne. Edited and Annotated by the Author of "The Gentle Life."

The Gentle Life. 2nd Series.

The Silent Hour: Essays, Original and Selected. By the Author of "The Gentle Life."

Half-Length Portraits. Short Studies of Notable Persons. By J. HAIN FRISWELL.

Essays on English Writers, for the Self-improvement of Students in English Literature.

Other People's Windows. By J. HAIN FRISWELL. 6s.

A Man's Thoughts. By J. HAIN FRISWELL.

The Countess of Pembroke's Arcadia. By Sir PHILIP SIDNEY. New Edition, 6s.

George Eliot: a Critical Study of her Life. By G. W. COOKE. Crown 8vo, 10s. 6d.

Germany. By S. BARING-GOULD. Crown 8vo, 3s. 6d.

Gilder (W. H.) Ice-Pack and Tundra. An Account of the Search for the "Jeannette." 8vo, 18s.

——— *Schwatka's Search.* Sledging in quest of the Franklin Records. Illustrated, 8vo, 12s. 6d.

Gilpin's Forest Scenery. Edited by F. G. HEATH. Post 8vo, 7s. 6d.

Gisborne (W.) New Zealand Rulers and Statesmen. With Portraits. Crown 8vo,

Gordon (General) Private Diary in China. Edited by S. MOSSMAN. Crown 8vo, 7s. 6d.

Gordon (J. E. H., B.A. Cantab.) Four Lectures on Electric Induction at the Royal Institution, 1878-9. Illust., square 16mo, 3s.

——— *Electric Lighting.* Illustrated, 8vo, 18s.

——— *Physical Treatise on Electricity and Magnetism.* 2nd Edition, enlarged, with coloured, full-page, &c., Illust. 2 vols., 8vo, 42s.

——— *Electricity for Schools.* Illustrated. Crown 8vo, 5s.

Gouffé (Jules) Royal Cookery Book. Translated and adapted for English use by ALPHONSE GOUFFÉ, Head Pastrycook to the Queen. New Edition, with plates in colours, Woodcuts, &c., 8vo, gilt edges, 42s.

——— Domestic Edition, half-bound, 10s. 6d.

Grant (General, U.S.) Personal Memoirs. With numerous Illustrations, Maps, &c. 2 vols., 8vo, 28s.

Great Artists. See "Biographies."

Great Musicians. Edited by F. HUEFFER. A Series of Biographies, crown 8vo, 3s. each:—

Bach.	Handel.	Purcell.
*Beethoven.	Haydn.	Rossini.
*Berlioz.	*Marcello.	Schubert.
English Church Composers. By BARETT.	Mendelssohn.	Schumann.
	Mozart.	Richard Wagner.
*Glück.	*Palestrina.	Weber.

* *In preparation.*

*Groves (J. Percy) Charmouth Grange: a Tale of the Seven-*teenth Century. Illustrated, small post 8vo, gilt, 6s.; plainer, 5s.

Guizot's History of France. Translated by ROBERT BLACK. Super-royal 8vo, very numerous Full-page and other Illustrations. In 8 vols., cloth extra, gilt, each 24s. This work is re-issued in cheaper binding, 8 vols., at 10s. 6d. each.

"It supplies a want which has long been felt, and ought to be in the hands of all students of history."—*Times.*

―――――――――――――――― *Masson's School Edition.* Abridged from the Translation by Robert Black, with Chronological Index, Historical and Genealogical Tables, &c. By Professor GUSTAVE MASSON, B.A. With 24 full-page Portraits, and other Illustrations. 1 vol., 8vo, 600 pp., 10s. 6d.

Guizot's History of England. In 3 vols. of about 500 pp. each, containing 60 to 70 full-page and other Illustrations, cloth extra, gilt, 24s. each; re-issue in cheaper binding, 10s. 6d. each.

"For luxury of typography, plainness of print, and beauty of illustration, these volumes, of which but one has as yet appeared in English, will hold their own against any production of an age so luxurious as our own in everything, typography not excepted."—*Times.*

Guyon (Mde.) Life. By UPHAM. 6th Edition, crown 8vo, 6s.

HALFORD (F. M.) *Floating Flies, and how to Dress them.* Coloured plates. 8vo, 15s.; large paper, 30s.

Hall (W. W.) How to Live Long; or, 1408 *Health Maxims,* Physical, Mental, and Moral. 2nd Edition, small post 8vo, 2s.

Hamilton (E.) Recollections of Fly-fishing for Salmon, Trout, and Grayling. With their Habits, Haunts, and History. Illustrated, small post 8vo, 6s.; large paper (100 numbered copies), 10s. 6d.

Hands (T.) Numerical Exercises in Chemistry. Cr. 8vo, 2s. 6d. and 2s.; Answers separately, 6d.

Hardy (Thomas). See LOW'S STANDARD NOVELS.

Hargreaves (Capt.) Voyage round Great Britain. Illustrated. Crown 8vo, 5s.

Harland (Marian) Home Kitchen: a Collection of Practical and Inexpensive Receipts. Crown 8vo, 5s.

Harper's Monthly Magazine. Published Monthly. 160 pages, fully Illustrated. 1s.
    Vol. I. December, 1880, to May, 1881.
    ,, II. June to November, 1881.
    ,, III. December, 1881, to May, 1882.
    ,, IV. June to November, 1882.
    ,, V. December, 1882, to May, 1883.
    ,, VI. June to November, 1883.
    ,, VII. December, 1883, to May, 1884.
    ,, VIII. June to November, 1884.
    ,, IX. December, 1884, to May, 1885.
    ,, X. June to November, 1885.
Super-royal 8vo, 8s. 6d. each.

    "'Harper's Magazine' is so thickly sown with excellent illustrations that to count them would be a work of time; not that it is a picture magazine, for the engravings illustrate the text after the manner seen in some of our choicest *éditions de luxe*."—*St. James's Gazette.*
    "It is so pretty, so big, and so cheap. . . . An extraordinary shillingsworth— 160 large octavo pages, with over a score of articles, and more than three times as many illustrations."—*Edinburgh Daily Review.*
    "An amazing shillingsworth . . . combining choice literature of both nations."—*Nonconformist.*

Harper's Young People. Vol. I., profusely Illustrated with woodcuts and 12 coloured plates. Royal 4to, extra binding, 7s. 6d.; gilt edges, 8s. Published Weekly, in wrapper, 1d. 12mo. Annual Subscription, post free, 6s. 6d.; Monthly, in wrapper, with coloured plate, 6d.; Annual Subscription, post free, 7s. 6d.

Harrison (Mary) Skilful Cook: a Practical Manual of Modern Experience. Crown 8vo, 5s.

Hatton (F.) North Borneo. With Biographical Sketch by Jos. HATTON. Illustrated from Original Drawings, Map, &c. 8vo, 18s.

Hatton (Joseph) Journalistic London: with Engravings and Portraits of Distinguished Writers of the Day. Fcap. 4to, 12s. 6d.

—— *Three Recruits, and the Girls they left behind them.* Small post 8vo, 6s.
    "It hurries us along in unflagging excitement."—*Times.*

Heath (Francis George) Autumnal Leaves. New Edition, with Coloured Plates in Facsimile from Nature. Crown 8vo, 14s.

—— *Fern Paradise.* New Edition, with Plates and Photos., crown 8vo, 12s. 6d.

Heath (Francis George) Fern World. With Nature-printed Coloured Plates. Crown 8vo, gilt edges, 12s. 6d. Cheap Edition, 6s.

—— *Gilpin's Forest Scenery.* Illustrated, 8vo, 12s. 6d.; New Edition, 7s. 6d.

—— *Our Woodland Trees.* With Coloured Plates and Engravings. Small 8vo, 12s. 6d.

—— *Peasant Life in the West of England.* New Edition, crown 8vo, 10s. 6d.

—— *Sylvan Spring.* With Coloured, &c., Illustrations. 12s. 6d.

—— *Trees and Ferns.* Illustrated, crown 8vo, 3s. 6d.

Heldmann (Bernard) Mutiny on Board the Ship "Leander." Small post 8vo, gilt edges, numerous Illustrations, 5s.

Henty (G. A.) Winning his Spurs. Illustrations. Cr. 8vo, 5s.

—— *Cornet of Horse: A Story for Boys.* Illust., cr. 8vo, 5s.

—— *Jack Archer: Tale of the Crimea.* Illust., crown 8vo, 5s.

Herrick (Robert) Poetry. Preface by AUSTIN DOBSON. With numerous Illustrations by E. A. ABBEY. 4to, gilt edges, 42s.

Hill (Staveley, Q.C., M.P.) From Home to Home: Two Long Vacations at the Foot of the Rocky Mountains. With Wood Engravings and Photogravures. 8vo, 21s.

Hitchman, Public Life of the Right Hon. Benjamin Disraeli, Earl of Beaconsfield. 3rd Edition, with Portrait. Crown 8vo, 3s. 6d.

Holmes (O. Wendell) Poetical Works. 2 vols., 18mo, exquisitely printed, and chastely bound in limp cloth, gilt tops, 10s. 6d.

Homer. Iliad, done into English Verse. By A. S. WAY. 5s.

Hudson (W. H.) The Purple Land that England Lost. Travels and Adventures in the Banda-Oriental, South America. 2 vols, crown 8vo, 21s.

Hundred Greatest Men (The). 8 portfolios, 21s. each, or 4 vols., half-morocco, gilt edges, 10 guineas. New Ed., 1 vol., royal 8vo, 21s.

Hygiene and Public Health. Edited by A. H. BUCK, M.D. Illustrated. 2 vols., royal 8vo, 42s.

Hymnal Companion of Common Prayer. See BICKERSTETH.

List of Publications. 15

ILLUSTRATED Text-Books of Art-Education. Edited by EDWARD J. POYNTER, R.A. Each Volume contains numerous Illustrations, and is strongly bound for Students, price 5s. Now ready:—

PAINTING.

Classic and Italian. By PERCY R. HEAD.
German, Flemish, and Dutch.
French and Spanish.
English and American.

ARCHITECTURE.

Classic and Early Christian.
Gothic and Renaissance. By T. ROGER SMITH.

SCULPTURE.

Antique: Egyptian and Greek.

Index to the English Catalogue, Jan., 1874, *to Dec.,* 1880. Royal 8vo, half-morocco, 18s.

Indian Garden Series. See ROBINSON (PHIL.).

Irving (Henry) Impressions of America. By J. HATTON. 2 vols., 21s.; New Edition, 1 vol., 6s.

Irving (Washington). Complete Library Edition of his Works in 27 Vols., Copyright, Unabridged, and with the Author's Latest Revisions, called the "Geoffrey Crayon" Edition, handsomely printed in large square 8vo, on superfine laid paper. Each volume, of about 500 pages, fully Illustrated. 12s. 6d. per vol. *See also* "Little Britain."

—————————— ("American Men of Letters.") 2s. 6d.

JAMES (C.) Curiosities of Law and Lawyers. 8vo, 7s. 6d.

Japan. See AUDSLEY.

Jerdon (Gertrude) Key-hole Country. Illustrated. Crown 8vo, cloth, 5s.

Johnston (H. H.) River Congo, from its Mouth to Bolobo. New Edition, 8vo, 21s.

Jones (Major) The Emigrants' Friend. A Complete Guide to the United States. New Edition. 2s. 6d.

Joyful Lays. Sunday School Song Book. By LOWRY and DOANE. Boards, 2s.

Julien (F.) English Student's French Examiner. 16mo, 2s.

—————— *First Lessons in Conversational French Grammar.* Crown 8vo, 1s.

Julien (F.) French at Home and at School. Book I., Accidence, &c. Square crown 8vo, 2s.

—————— *Conversational French Reader.* 16mo, cloth, 2s. 6d.

—————— *Petites Leçons de Conversation et de Grammaire.* New Edition, 3s.

—————— *Phrases of Daily Use.* Limp cloth, 6d.

KELSEY *(C. B.) Diseases of the Rectum and Anus.* Illustrated. 8vo, 18s.

Kempis (Thomas à) Daily Text-Book. Square 16mo, 2s. 6d.; interleaved as a Birthday Book, 3s. 6d.

Kershaw (S. W.) Protestants from France in their English Home. Crown 8vo, 6s.

Kielland. Skipper Worsé. By the Earl of Ducie. Cr. 8vo, 10s. 6d.

Kingston (W. H. G.) Dick Cheveley. Illustrated, 16mo, gilt edges, 7s. 6d.; plainer binding, plain edges, 5s.

—————— *Heir of Kilfinnan.* Uniform, 7s. 6d.; also 5s.

—————— *Snow-Shoes and Canoes.* Uniform, 7s. 6d.; also 5s.

—————— *Two Supercargoes.* Uniform, 7s. 6d.; also 5s.

—————— *With Axe and Rifle.* Uniform, 7s. 6d.; also 5s.

Knight (E. F.) Albania and Montenegro. Illust. 8vo, 12s. 6d.

Knight (E. J.) Cruise of the "Falcon." A Voyage round the World in a 30-Ton Yacht. Illust. New Ed. 2 vols., crown 8vo, 24s.

LANIER *(Sidney) Boy's Froissart.* Illustrated, crown 8vo, gilt edges, 7s. 6d.

—————— *Boy's King Arthur.* Uniform, 7s. 6d.

—————— *Boy's Mabinogion; Original Welsh Legends of King Arthur.* Uniform, 7s. 6d.

—————— *Boy's Percy: Ballads of Love and Adventure, selected from the "Reliques."* Uniform, 7s. 6d.

Lansdell (H.) Through Siberia. 2 vols., 8vo, 30s.; 1 vol., 10s. 6d.

—— *Russia in Central Asia.* Illustrated. 2 vols, 42s.

Larden (W.) School Course on Heat. Second Edition, Illustrated, crown 8vo, 5s.

Lenormant (F.) Beginnings of History. Crown 8vo, 12s. 6d.

Leonardo da Vinci's Literary Works. Edited by Dr. JEAN PAUL RICHTER. Containing his Writings on Painting, Sculpture, and Architecture, his Philosophical Maxims, Humorous Writings, and Miscellaneous Notes on Personal Events, on his Contemporaries, on Literature, &c.; published from Manuscripts. 2 vols., imperial 8vo, containing about 200 Drawings in Autotype Reproductions, and numerous other Illustrations. Twelve Guineas.

Library of Religious Poetry. Best Poems of all Ages. Edited by SCHAFF and GILMAN. Royal 8vo, 21s.; re-issue in cheaper binding, 10s. 6d.

Lindsay (W. S.) History of Merchant Shipping. Over 150 Illustrations, Maps, and Charts. In 4 vols., demy 8vo, cloth extra. Vols. 1 and 2, 11s. each; vols. 3 and 4, 14s. each. 4 vols., 50s.

Little Britain, The Spectre Bridegroom, and *Legend of Sleeepy Hollow.* By WASHINGTON IRVING. An entirely New *Edition de luxe.* Illustrated by 120 very fine Engravings on Wood, by Mr. J. D. COOPER. Designed by Mr. CHARLES O. MURRAY. Re-issue, square crown 8vo, cloth, 6s.

Long (Mrs.) Peace and War in the Transvaal. 12mo, 3s. 6d.

Lowell (J. R.) Life of Nathaniel Hawthorn.

Low (Sampson, Jun.) Sanitary Suggestions. Illustrated, crown 8vo, 2s. 6d.

Low's Standard Library of Travel and Adventure. Crown 8vo, uniform in cloth extra, 7s. 6d., except where price is given.
  1. **The Great Lone Land.** By Major W. F. BUTLER, C.B.
  2. **The Wild North Land.** By Major W. F. BUTLER, C.B.
  3. **How I found Livingstone.** By H. M. STANLEY.
  4. **Through the Dark Continent.** By H. M. STANLEY. 12s. 6d.
  5. **The Threshold of the Unknown Region.** By C. R. MARKHAM. (4th Edition, with Additional Chapters, 10s. 6d.)
  6. **Cruise of the Challenger.** By W. J. J. SPRY, R.N.
  7. **Burnaby's On Horseback through Asia Minor.** 10s. 6d.
  8. **Schweinfurth's Heart of Africa.** 2 vols., 15s.
  9. **Marshall's Through America.**
  10. **Lansdell's Through Siberia.** Illustrated and unabridged, 10s. 6d.

Low's Standard Novels. Small post 8vo, cloth extra, 6s. each, unless otherwise stated.

A Daughter of Heth. By W. BLACK.
In Silk Attire. By W. BLACK.
Kilmeny. A Novel. By W. BLACK.
Lady Silverdale's Sweetheart. By W. BLACK.
Sunrise. By W. BLACK.
Three Feathers. By WILLIAM BLACK.
Alice Lorraine. By R. D. BLACKMORE.
Christowell, a Dartmoor Tale. By R. D. BLACKMORE.
Clara Vaughan. By R. D. BLACKMORE.
Cradock Nowell. By R. D. BLACKMORE.
Cripps the Carrier. By R. D. BLACKMORE.
Erema; or, My Father's Sin. By R. D. BLACKMORE.
Lorna Doone. By R. D. BLACKMORE.
Mary Anerley. By R. D. BLACKMORE.
Tommy Upmore. By R. D. BLACKMORE.
An English Squire. By Miss COLERIDGE.
A Story of the Dragonnades; or, Asylum Christi. By the Rev. E. GILLIAT, M.A.
A Laodicean. By THOMAS HARDY.
Far from the Madding Crowd. By THOMAS HARDY.
Pair of Blue Eyes. By THOMAS HARDY.
Return of the Native. By THOMAS HARDY.
The Hand of Ethelberta. By THOMAS HARDY.
The Trumpet Major. By THOMAS HARDY.
Two on a Tower. By THOMAS HARDY.
Three Recruits. By JOSEPH HATTON.
A Golden Sorrow. By Mrs. CASHEL HOEY. New Edition.
Out of Court. By Mrs. CASHEL HOEY.
Adela Cathcart. By GEORGE MAC DONALD.
Guild Court. By GEORGE MAC DONALD.
Mary Marston. By GEORGE MAC DONALD.
Stephen Archer. New Ed. of "Gifts." By GEORGE MAC DONALD.
The Vicar's Daughter. By GEORGE MAC DONALD.
Weighed and Wanting. By GEORGE MAC DONALD.
Diane. By Mrs. MACQUOID.
Elinor Dryden. By Mrs. MACQUOID.
My Lady Greensleeves. By HELEN MATHERS.
Alaric Spenceley. By Mrs. J. H. RIDDELL.
Daisies and Buttercups. By Mrs. J. H. RIDDELL.
The Senior Partner. By Mrs. J. H. RIDDELL.
A Struggle for Fame. By Mrs. J. H. RIDDELL.
Jack's Courtship. By W. CLARK RUSSELL.
John Holdsworth. By W. CLARK RUSSELL.
A Sailor's Sweetheart. By W. CLARK RUSSELL.
Sea Queen. By W. CLARK RUSSELL.
Watch Below. By W. CLARK RUSSELL.
Wreck of the Grosvenor. By W. CLARK RUSSELL.

Low's Standard Novels—*continued.*
   The **Lady Maud.** By W. CLARK RUSSELL.
   Little Loo. By W. CLARK RUSSELL.
   My Wife and I. By Mrs. BEECHER STOWE.
   Poganuc People, their Loves and Lives. By Mrs. B. STOWE.
   Ben Hur: a Tale of the Christ. By LEW. WALLACE.
   Anne. By CONSTANCE FENIMORE WOOLSON.
   For the Major. By CONSTANCE FENIMORE WOOLSON. 5*s.*
   French Heiress in her own Chateau.

Low's Handbook to the Charities of London. Edited and revised to date by C. MACKESON, F.S.S., Editor of "A Guide to the Churches of London and its Suburbs," &c. Yearly, 1*s.* 6*d.*; Paper, 1*s.*

Lyne (*Charles*) *New Guinea.* Illustrated, crown 8vo, 10*s.* 6*d.* An Account of the Establishment of the British Protectorate over the Southern Shores of New Guinea.

*M*c*CORMICK* (*R.*). *Voyages of Discovery in the Arctic and Antarctic Seas* in the "Erebus" and "Terror," in Search of Sir John Franklin, &c., with Autobiographical Notice by the Author, who was Medical Officer to each Expedition. With Maps and Lithographic, &c., Illustrations. 2 vols., royal 8vo, 52*s.* 6*d.*

MacDonald (*G.*) *Orts.* Small post 8vo, 6*s.*

———— See also "Low's Standard Novels."

Macgregor (*John*) "*Rob Roy*" *on the Baltic.* 3rd Edition, small post 8vo, 2*s.* 6*d.*; cloth, gilt edges, 3*s.* 6*d.*

———— *A Thousand Miles in the* "*Rob Roy*" *Canoe.* 11th Edition, small post 8vo, 2*s.* 6*d.*; cloth, gilt edges, 3*s.* 6*d.*

———— *Voyage Alone in the Yawl* "*Rob Roy.*" New Edition, with additions, small post 8vo, 5*s.*; 3*s.* 6*d.* and 2*s.* 6*d.*

Macquoid (*Mrs.*). See LOW'S STANDARD NOVELS.

Magazine. See DECORATION, ENGLISH ETCHINGS, HARPER.

Maginn (*W.*) *Miscellanies. Prose and Verse. With Memoir.* 2 vols., crown 8vo, 24*s.*

Manitoba. See BRYCE.

Manning (E. F.) Delightful Thames. Illustrated. 4to, fancy boards, 5s.

Markham (C. R.) The Threshold of the Unknown Region. Crown 8vo, with Four Maps. 4th Edition. Cloth extra, 10s. 6d.

—— *War between Peru and Chili,* 1879-1881. Third Ed. Crown 8vo, with Maps, 10s. 6d.

—— See also "Foreign Countries."

Marshall (W. G.) Through America. New Ed., cr. 8vo, 7s. 6d.

Martin (J. W.) Float Fishing and Spinning in the Nottingham Style. New Edition. Crown 8vo, 2s. 6d.

Maury (Commander) Physical Geography of the Sea, and its Meteorology. New Edition, with Charts and Diagrams, cr. 8vo, 6s.

Men of Mark: a Gallery of Contemporary Portraits of the most Eminent Men of the Day, specially taken from Life. Complete in Seven Vols., 4to, handsomely bound, cloth, gilt edges, 25s. each.

Mendelssohn Family (The), 1729—1847. From Letters and Journals. Translated. New Edition, 2 vols., 8vo, 30s.

Mendelssohn. See also "Great Musicians."

Merrifield's Nautical Astronomy. Crown 8vo, 7s. 6d.

Millard (H. B.) Bright's Disease of the Kidneys. Illustrated. 8vo, 12s. 6d.

Mitchell (D. G.; Ik. Marvel) Works. Uniform Edition, small 8vo, 5s. each.

Bound together.	Reveries of a Bachelor.
Doctor Johns.	Seven Stories, Basement and Attic.
Dream Life.	Wet Days at Edgewood.
Out-of-Town Places.	

Mitford (Mary Russell) Our Village. With 12 full-page and 157 smaller Cuts. Cr. 4to, cloth, gilt edges, 21s.; cheaper binding, 10s. 6d.

Mollett (J. W.) Illustrated Dictionary of Words used in Art and Archæology. Terms in Architecture, Arms, Bronzes, Christian Art, Colour, Costume, Decoration, Devices, Emblems, Heraldry, Lace, Personal Ornaments, Pottery, Painting, Sculpture, &c. Small 4to, 15s.

Morley (H.) English Literature in the Reign of Victoria. 2000th volume of the Tauchnitz Collection of Authors. 18mo, 2s. 6d.

Morwood (V. S.) Our Gipsies in City, Tent, and Van. 8vo, 18s.

Muller (E.) Noble Words and Noble Deeds. By PHILIPPOTEAUX. Square imperial 16mo, cloth extra, 7s. 6d.; plainer binding, 5s.

Music. See "Great Musicians."

NEW Zealand. See BRADSHAW.

New Zealand Rulers and Statesmen. See GISBORNE.

Newbiggin's Sketches and Tales. 18mo, 4s.

Nicholls (J. H. Kerry) The King Country: Explorations in New Zealand. Many Illustrations and Map. New Edition, 8vo, 21s.

Nicholson (C.) Work and Workers of the British Association. 12mo, 1s.

Nixon (J.) Complete Story of the Transvaal. 8vo, 12s. 6d.

Nordhoff (C.) California, for Health, Pleasure, and Residence. New Edition, 8vo, with Maps and Illustrations, 12s. 6d.

Northbrook Gallery. Edited by Lord Ronald Gower. 36 Permanent Photographs. Imperial 4to, 63s.; large paper, 105s.

Nursery Playmates (Prince of). 217 Coloured Pictures for Children by eminent Artists. Folio, in coloured boards, 6s.

O'BRIEN (R. B.) Fifty Years of Concessions to Ireland. With a Portrait of T. Drummond. Vol. I., 16s.; II., 16s.

Orvis (C. F.) Fishing with the Fly. Illustrated. 8vo, 12s. 6d.

Our Little Ones in Heaven. Edited by the Rev. H. ROBBINS. With Frontispiece after Sir JOSHUA REYNOLDS. New Edition, 5s.

Owen (Douglas) Marine Insurance Notes and Clauses. New Edition, 14s.

PALLISER (Mrs.) A History of Lace. New Edition, with additional cuts and text. 8vo, 21s.

—— *The China Collector's Pocket Companion.* With upwards of 1000 Illustrations of Marks and Monograms. Small 8vo, 5s.

Pascoe (C. E.) London of To-Day. Illust., crown 8vo, 3s. 6d.

Pharmacopœia of the United States of America. 8vo, 21s.

Philpot (H. J.) Diabetes Mellitus. Crown 8vo, 5s.

—— *Diet System.* Three Tables, in cases, 1s. each.

Pinto (Major Serpa) How I Crossed Africa. With 24 full-page and 118 half-page and smaller Illustrations, 13 small Maps, and 1 large one. 2 vols., 8vo, 42*s.*

Plunkett (Major G. F.) Primer of Orthographic Projection. Elementary Practical Solid Geometry clearly explained. With Problems and Exercises. Specially adapted for Science and Art Classes, and for Students who have not the aid of a Teacher.

Poe (E. A.) The Raven. Illustr. by DORÉ. Imperial folio, 63*s.*

Poems of the Inner Life. Chiefly from Modern Authors. Small 8vo, 5*s.*

Polar Expeditions. See GILDER, MARKHAM, MCCORMICK.

Porter (Noah) Elements of Moral Science. 10*s.* 6*d.*

Powell (W.) Wanderings in a Wild Country; or, Three Years among the Cannibals of New Britain. Illustr., 8vo, 18*s.*; cr. 8vo, 5*s.*

Power (Frank) Letters from Khartoum during the Siege. Fcap. 8vo, boards, 1*s.*

Poynter (Edward J., R.A.). See " Illustrated Text-books."

Publishers' Circular (The), and General Record of British ana Foreign Literature. Published on the 1st and 15th of every Month, 3*d.*

*R*EBER *(F.) History of Ancient Art.* 8vo, 18*s.*

Redford (G.) Ancient Sculpture. Crown 8vo, 5*s.*

Richter (Dr. Jean Paul) Italian Art in the National Gallery. 4to. Illustrated. Cloth gilt, 2*l.* 2*s.*; half-morocco, uncut, 2*l.* 12*s.* 6*d.*

—— See also LEONARDO DA VINCI.

Riddell (Mrs. J. H.) See LOW's STANDARD NOVELS.

Robin Hood; Merry Adventures of. Written and illustrated by HOWARD PYLE. Imperial 8vo, 15*s.*

Robinson (Phil.) In my Indian Garden. Crown 8vo, limp cloth, 3*s.* 6*d.*

Robinson (Phil.) Indian Garden Series. 1s. 6d.; boards, 1s. each.
I. Chasing a Fortune, &c. : Stories.   II. Tigers at Large.

—— *Noah's Ark. A Contribution to the Study of Unnatural* History.   Small post 8vo, 12s. 6d.

—— *Sinners and Saints : a Tour across the United States of* America, and Round them.   Crown 8vo, 10s. 6d.

—— *Under the Punkah.*   Crown 8vo, limp cloth, 5s.

Rockstro (W. S.) History of Music.

Rodrigues (J. C.) The Panama Canal.   Crown 8vo, cloth extra, 5s.
> "A series of remarkable articles ... a mine of valuable data for editors and diplomatists."—*New York Nation.*

Roland; the Story of.   Crown 8vo, illustrated, 6s.

Rose (J.) Complete Practical Machinist.   New Ed., 12mo, 12s. 6d.

—— *Mechanical Drawing.*   Illustrated, small 4to, 16s.

Rose Library (The).   Popular Literature of all Countries.   Each volume, 1s.; cloth, 2s. 6d.   Many of the Volumes are Illustrated—
Little Women.   By LOUISA M. ALCOTT.
Little Women Wedded.   Forming a Sequel to "Little Women."
Little Women and Little Women Wedded.   1 vol., cloth gilt, 3s. 6d.
Little Men.   By L. M. ALCOTT.   2s.; cloth gilt, 3s. 6d.
An Old-Fashioned Girl.   By LOUISA M. ALCOTT.   2s.; cloth, 3s. 6d.
Work.   A Story of Experience.   By L. M. ALCOTT.   3s. 6d.; 2 vols. 1s. each.
Stowe (Mrs. H. B.) The Pearl of Orr's Island.
—— **The Minister's Wooing.**
—— **We and our Neighbours.**   2s.; cloth gilt, 6s.
—— **My Wife and I.**   2s.; cloth gilt, 6s.
Hans Brinker; or, the Silver Skates.   By Mrs. DODGE.
My Study Windows.   By J. R. LOWELL.
The Guardian Angel.   By OLIVER WENDELL HOLMES.
My Summer in a Garden.   By C. D. WARNER.
Dred.   By Mrs. BEECHER STOWE.   2s.; cloth gilt, 3s. 6d.
Farm Ballads.   By WILL CARLETON.
Farm Festivals.   By WILL CARLETON.

Rose Library (The)—continued.

    Farm Legends. By WILL CARLETON.

    The Clients of Dr. Bernagius. 3*s*. 6*d*.; 2 parts, 1*s*. each.

    The Undiscovered Country. By W. D. HOWELLS. 3*s*. 6*d*. and 1*s*.

    Baby Rue. By C. M. CLAY. 3*s*. 6*d*. and 1*s*.

    The Rose in Bloom. By L. M. ALCOTT. 2*s*.; cloth gilt, 3*s*. 6*d*.

    Eight Cousins. By L. M. ALCOTT. 2*s*.; cloth gilt, 3*s*. 6*d*.

    Under the Lilacs. By L. M. ALCOTT. 2*s*.; also 3*s*. 6*d*.

    Silver Pitchers. By LOUISA M. ALCOTT. 3*s*. 6*d*. and 1*s*.

    Jimmy's Cruise in the "Pinafore," and other Tales. By LOUISA M. ALCOTT. 2*s*.; cloth gilt, 3*s*. 6*d*.

    Jack and Jill. By LOUISA M. ALCOTT. 5*s*.; 2*s*.

    Hitherto. By the Author of the "Gayworthys." 2 vols., 1*s*. each; 1 vol., cloth gilt, 3*s*. 6*d*.

    Friends: a Duet. By E. STUART PHELPS. 3*s*. 6*d*.

    A Gentleman of Leisure. A Novel. By EDGAR FAWCETT. 3*s*. 6*d*.; 1*s*.

    The Story of Helen Troy. 3*s*. 6*d*.; also 1*s*.

Ross (Mars; and Stonehewer Cooper) Highlands of Cantabria; or, Three Days from England. Illustrations and Map, 8vo, 21*s*.

Round the Yule Log: Norwegian Folk and Fairy Tales. Translated from the Norwegian of P. CHR. ASBJÖRNSEN. With 100 Illustrations after drawings by Norwegian Artists, and an Introduction by E. W. Gosse. Impl. 16mo, cloth extra, gilt edges, 7*s*. 6*d*. and 5*s*.

Rousselet (Louis) Son of the Constable of France. Small post 8vo, numerous Illustrations, 5*s*.

  ——— *King of the Tigers: a Story of Central India.* Illustrated. Small post 8vo, gilt, 6*s*.; plainer, 5*s*.

  ——— *Drummer Boy.* Illustrated. Small post 8vo, 5*s*.

Rowbotham (F.) Trip to Prairie Land. The Shady Side of Emigration. 5*s*.

Russell (W. Clark) English Channel Ports and the Estate of the East and West India Dock Company. Crown 8vo, 1*s*.

  ——— *Jack's Courtship.* 3 vols., 31*s*. 6*d*.; 1 vol., 6*s*.

Russell (W. Clark) The Lady Maud.   3 vols., 31s. 6d.;   1 vol., 6s.

———— *Little Loo.*   New Edition, small post 8vo, 6s.

———— *My Watch Below; or, Yarns Spun when off Duty.*   Small post 8vo, 6s.

———— *Sailor's Language.*   Illustrated.   Crown 8vo, 3s. 6d.

———— *Sea Queen.*   3 vols., 31s. 6d.;   1 vol., 6s.

———— *Strange Voyage.*   Nautical Novel.   3 vols., crown 8vo, 31s. 6d.

———— *Wreck of the Grosvenor.*   4to, sewed, 6d.

———— See also LOW'S STANDARD NOVELS.

SAINTS and their Symbols: A Companion in the Churches and Picture Galleries of Europe. Illustrated. Royal 16mo, 3s. 6d.

Salisbury (Lord) Life and Speeches.   By F. S. Pulling, M.A. With Photogravure Portrait of Lord Salisbury. 2 vols., crown 8vo, 21s.

Saunders (A.) Our Domestic Birds: Poultry in England and New Zealand. Crown 8vo, 6s.

Scherr (Prof. J.) History of English Literature. Cr. 8vo, 8s. 6d.

Schley. Rescue of Greely. Maps and Illustrations, 8vo, 12s. 6d.

Schuyler (Eugène). The Life of Peter the Great.   By EUGÈNE SCHUYLER, Author of "Turkestan." 2 vols., 8vo, 32s.

Schweinfurth (Georg) Heart of Africa.   Three Years' Travels and Adventures in the Unexplored Regions of Central Africa, from 1868 to 1871. Illustrations and large Map. 2 vols., crown 8vo, 15s.

Scott (Leader) Renaissance of Art in Italy.   4to, 31s. 6d.

Sea, River, and Creek.   By GARBOARD STREYKE.   *The Eastern* Coast. 12mo, 1s.

Senior (W.) Waterside Sketches. Imp. 32mo, 1s.6d., boards, 1s.

Shadbolt and Mackinnon's South African Campaign, 1879. Containing a portrait and biography of every officer who lost his life. 4to, handsomely bound, 2l. 10s.

Shadbolt (S. H.) Afghan Campaigns of 1878—1880. By SYDNEY SHADBOLT. 2 vols., royal quarto, cloth extra, 3*l.*

Shakespeare. Edited by R. GRANT WHITE. 3 vols., crown 8vo, gilt top, 36*s.*; *Édition de luxe*, 6 vols., 8vo, cloth extra, 63*s.*

Shakespeare. See also WHITE (R. GRANT).

"*Shooting Niagara;*" *or, The Last Days of Caucusia.* By the Author of "The New Democracy." Small post 8vo, boards, 1*s.*

Sidney (Sir Philip) Arcadia. New Edition, 6*s.*

Siegfried : The Story of. Illustrated, crown 8vo, cloth, 6*s.*

Sinclair (Mrs.) Indigenous Flowers of the Hawaiian Islands. 44 Plates in Colour. Imp. folio, extra binding, gilt edges, 31*s.* 6*d.*

Sir Roger de Coverley. Re-imprinted from the "Spectator." With 125 Woodcuts and special steel Frontispiece. Small fcap. 4to, 6*s.*

Smith (G.) Assyrian Explorations and Discoveries. Illustrated by Photographs and Woodcuts. New Edition, demy 8vo, 18*s.*

—————— *The Chaldean Account of Genesis.* With many Illustrations. 16*s.* New Edition, revised and re-written by PROFESSOR SAYCE, Queen's College, Oxford. 8vo, 18*s.*

Smith (J. Moyr) Ancient Greek Female Costume. 112 full-page Plates and other Illustrations. Crown 8vo, 7*s.* 6*d.*

—————— *Hades of Ardenne: a Visit to the Caves of Han.* Crown 8vo, Illustrated, 5*s.*

—————— *Legendary Studies, and other Sketches for Decorative* Figure Panels. 7*s.* 6*d.*

—————— *Wooing of Æthra.* Illustrated. 32mo, 1*s.*

Smith (Sydney) Life and Times. By STUART J. REID. Illustrated. 8vo, 21*s.*

Smith (T. Roger) Architecture, Gothic and Renaissance. Illustrated, crown 8vo, 5*s.*

—————————————— *Classic and Early Christian.* Illustrated. Crown 8vo, 5*s.*

Smith (W. R.) Laws concerning Public Health. 8vo, 31*s.* 6*d.*

Somerset (Lady H.) Our Village Life. Words and Illustrations. Thirty Coloured Plates, royal 4to, fancy covers, 5s.

Spanish and French Artists. By GERARD SMITH. (Poynter's Art Text-books.) 5s.

Spiers' French Dictionary. 29th Edition, remodelled. 2 vols., 8vo, 18s.; half bound, 21s.

Spry (W. J. J., R.N.) Cruise of H.M.S. "Challenger." With many Illustrations. 6th Edition, 8vo, cloth, 18s. Cheap Edition, crown 8vo, 7s. 6d.

Spyri (Joh.) Heidi's Early Experiences: a Story for Children and those who love Children. Illustrated, small post 8vo, 4s. 6d.

—— *Heidi's Further Experiences.* Illust., sm. post 8vo, 4s. 6d.

Stanley (H. M.) Congo, and Founding its Free State. Illustrated, 2 vols., 8vo, 42s.

—— *How I Found Livingstone.* 8vo, 10s. 6d.; cr. 8vo, 7s. 6d.

—— *Through the Dark Continent.* Crown 8vo, 12s. 6d.

Stenhouse (Mrs.) An Englishwoman in Utah. Crown 8vo, 2s. 6d.

Stevens (E. W.) Fly-Fishing in Maine Lakes. 8s. 6d.

Stockton (Frank R.) The Story of Viteau. With 16 page Illustrations. Crown 8vo, 5s.

Stoker (Bram) Under the Sunset. Crown 8vo, 6s.

Stowe (Mrs. Beecher) Dred. Cloth, gilt edges, 3s. 6d.; boards, 2s.

—— *Little Foxes.* Cheap Ed., 1s.; Library Edition, 4s. 6d.

—— *My Wife and I.* Small post 8vo, 6s.

—— *Old Town Folk.* 6s.; Cheap Edition, 3s.

—— *Old Town Fireside Stories.* Cloth extra, 3s. 6d.

—— *We and our Neighbours.* Small post 8vo, 6s.

—— *Poganuc People: their Loves and Lives.* Crown 8vo, 6s.

—— *Chimney Corner.* 1s.; cloth, 1s. 6d.

—— See also ROSE LIBRARY.

Sullivan (A. M.) Nutshell History of Ireland. Paper boards, 6*d.*

Sutton (A. K.) A B C Digest of the Bankruptcy Law. 8vo, 3*s.* and 2*s.* 6*d.*

TAINE (H. A.) "Les Origines de la France Contemporaine." Translated by JOHN DURAND.
- I. The Ancient Regime.   Demy 8vo, cloth, 16*s.*
- II. The French Revolution.   Vol. 1.   do.
- III.   Do.   do.   Vol. 2.   do.
- IV.   Do.   do.   Vol. 3.   do.

Talbot (Hon. E.) A Letter on Emigration. 1*s.*

Tauchnitz's English Editions of German Authors. Each volume, cloth flexible, 2*s.*; or sewed, 1*s.* 6*d.* (Catalogues post free.)

Tauchnitz (B.) German and English Dictionary. 2*s.*; paper, 1*s.* 6*d.*; roan, 2*s.* 6*d.*

—— *French and English Dictionary.* 2*s.*; paper, 1*s.* 6*d.*; roan, 2*s.* 6*d.*

—— *Italian and English Dictionary.* 2*s.*; paper, 1*s.* 6*d.*; roan, 2*s.* 6*d.*

—— *Spanish and English.* 2*s.*; paper, 1*s.* 6*d.*; roan, 2*s.* 6*d.*

Taylor (W. M.) Paul the Missionary. Crown 8vo, 7*s.* 6*d.*

Thausing (Prof.) Malt and the Fabrication of Beer. 8vo, 45*s.*

Theakston (M.) British Angling Flies. Illustrated. Cr. 8vo, 5*s.*

Thomson (W.) Algebra for Colleges and Schools. With numerous Examples. 8vo, 5*s.*, Key, 1*s.* 6*d.*

Thomson (Jos.) Through Masai Land. Illustrations and Maps. 21*s.*

Thoreau. American Men of Letters. Crown 8vo, 2*s.* 6*d.*

Tolhausen (Alexandre) Grand Supplément du Dictionnaire Technologique. 3*s.* 6*d.*

Tristram (Rev. Canon) Pathways of Palestine: A Descriptive Tour through the Holy Land. First Series. Illustrated by 44 Permanent Photographs. 2 vols., folio, cloth extra, gilt edges, 31*s.* 6*d.* each.

Trollope (Anthony) Thompson Hall. 1s.

Tromholt (S.) Under the Rays of the Aurora Borealis. By C. SIEWERS. Photographs and Portraits. 2 vols., 8vo, 30s.

Tunis. See REID.

Turner (Edward) Studies in Russian Literature. Cr. 8vo, 8s. 6d.

UNION Jack (The). Every Boy's Paper. Edited by G. A. HENTY. Profusely Illustrated with Coloured and other Plates. Vol. I., 6s. Vols. II., III., IV., 7s. 6d. each.

VASILI (Count) Berlin Society. Translated. Cown 8vo, 6s.

—— *World of London (La Société de Londres).* Translated. Crown 8vo, 6s.

Velazquez and Murillo. By C. B. CURTIS. With Original Etchings. Royal 8vo, 31s. 6d.; large paper, 63s.

Victoria (Queen) Life of. By GRACE GREENWOOD. With numerous Illustrations. Small post 8vo, 6s.

Vincent (Mrs. Howard) Forty Thousand Miles over Land and Water. With Illustrations engraved under the direction of Mr. H. BLACKBURN. 2 vols, crown 8vo, 21s.

Viollet-le-Duc (E.) Lectures on Architecture. Translated by BENJAMIN BUCKNALL, Architect. With 33 Steel Plates and 200 Wood Engravings. Super-royal 8vo, leather back, gilt top, 2 vols., 3l. 3s.

Vivian (A. P.) Wanderings in the Western Land. 3rd Ed., 10s. 6d.

BOOKS BY JULES VERNE.

LARGE CROWN 8vo. WORKS.	Containing 350 to 600 pp. and from 50 to 100 full-page illustrations.		Containing the whole of the text with some illustrations	
	In very handsome cloth binding, gilt edges.	In plainer binding, plain edges.	In cloth binding, gilt edges, smaller type.	Coloured board
	s. d.	s. d.	s. d.	
20,000 Leagues under the Sea. Parts I. and II.	10 6	5 0	3 6	2 vols., 1s. eac
Hector Servadac	10 6	5 0	3 6	2 vols., 1s. eac
The Fur Country	10 6	5 0	3 6	2 vols., 1s. eac
The Earth to the Moon and a Trip round it	10 6	5 0	2 vols., 2s. ea.	2 vols., 1s. eac
Michael Strogoff	10 6	5 0	3 6	2 vols., 1s. eac
Dick Sands, the Boy Captain	10 6	5 0	3 6	2 vols., 1s. eac
Five Weeks in a Balloon	7 6	3 6	2 0	1s. 0d.
Adventures of Three Englishmen and Three Russians	7 6	3 6	2 0	1 0
Round the World in Eighty Days	7 6	3 6	2 0	1 0
A Floating City	7 6	3 6	2 0	1 0
The Blockade Runners			2 0	1 0
Dr. Ox's Experiment	—	—	2 0	1 0
A Winter amid the Ice			2 0	1 0
Survivors of the "Chancellor"	7 6	3 6	2 0	2 vols., 1s. eac
Martin Paz			2 0	1s. 0d.
The Mysterious Island, 3 vols.:—	22 6	10 6	6 0	3 0
I. Dropped from the Clouds	7 6	3 6	2 0	1 0
II. Abandoned	7 6	3 6	2 0	1 0
III. Secret of the Island	7 6	3 6	2 0	1 0
The Child of the Cavern	7 6	3 6	2 0	1 0
The Begum's Fortune	7 6	3 6	2 0	1 0
The Tribulations of a Chinaman	7 6	3 6	2 0	1 0
The Steam House, 2 vols.:—				
I. Demon of Cawnpore	7 6	3 6	2 0	1 0
II. Tigers and Traitors	7 6	3 6	2 0	1 0
The Giant Raft, 2 vols.:—				
I. 800 Leagues on the Amazon	7 6	3 6	2 0	1 0
II. The Cryptogram	7 6	3 6	2 0	1 0
The Green Ray	6 0	5 0	—	1 0
Godfrey Morgan	7 6	3 6	2 0	1 0
Kéraban the Inflexible:—				
I. Captain of the "Guidara"	7 6			
II. Scarpante the Spy	7 6			
The Archipelago on Fire	7 6			
The Vanished Diamond	7 6			

CELEBRATED TRAVELS AND TRAVELLERS. 3 vols. 8vo, 600 pp., 100 full-page illustrations, 12s. 6d. gilt edges, 14s. each:—(1) THE EXPLORATION OF THE WORLD. (2) THE GREAT NAVIGATORS OF THE EIGHTEENTH CENTURY. (3) THE GREAT EXPLORERS OF THE NINETEENTH CENTURY.

WAHL (W. H.) *Galvanoplastic Manipulation for the* Electro-Plater. 8vo, 35*s*.

Wallace (L.) *Ben Hur: A Tale of the Christ.* Crown 8vo, 6*s*.

Waller (Rev. C. H.) *The Names on the Gates of Pearl*, and other Studies. New Edition. Crown 8vo, cloth extra, 3*s*. 6*d*.

—— *A Grammar and Analytical Vocabulary of the Words in* the Greek Testament. Compiled from Brüder's Concordance. For the use of Divinity Students and Greek Testament Classes. Part I. Grammar. Small post 8vo, cloth, 2*s*. 6*d*. Part II. Vocabulary, 2*s*. 6*d*.

—— *Adoption and the Covenant.* Some Thoughts on Confirmation. Super-royal 16mo, cloth limp, 2*s*. 6*d*.

—— *Silver Sockets; and other Shadows of Redemption.* Sermons at Christ Church, Hampstead. Small post 8vo, 6*s*.

Walton (Iz.) *Wallet Book*, CIƆIƆLXXXV. 21*s*.; l. p. 42*s*.

Walton (T. H.) *Coal Mining.* With Illustrations. 4to, 25*s*.

Warder (G. W.) *Utopian Dreams and Lotus Leaves.* Crown 8vo, 6*s*.

Warner (C. D.) *My Summer in a Garden.* Boards, 1*s*.; leatherette, 1*s*. 6*d*.; cloth, 2*s*.

Warren (W. F.) *Paradise Found; the North Pole the Cradle* of the Human Race. Illustrated. Crown 8vo, 12*s*. 6*d*.

Washington Irving's Little Britain. Square crown 8vo, 6*s*.

Watson (P. B.) *Marcus Aurelius Antoninus.* Portr. 8vo, 15*s*.

Webster. (American Men of Letters.) 18mo, 2*s*. 6*d*.

Weir (Harrison) *Animal Stories, Old and New, told in Pic*tures and Prose. Coloured, &c., Illustrations. 56 pp., 4to, 5*s*.

Wells (H. P.) *Fly Rods and Fly Tackle.* Illustrated. 10*s*. 6*d*.

Wheatley (H. B.) and *Delamotte* (P. H.) *Art Work in Porce*lain. Large 8vo, 2*s*. 6*d*.

—— *Art Work in Gold and Silver. Modern.* Large 8vo, 2*s*. 6*d*.

—— *Handbook of Decorative Art.* 10*s*. 6*d*.

Whisperings. Poems. Small post 8vo, cloth extra, gilt edges, 3*s*. 6*d*.

White (R. Grant) *England Without and Within.* Crown 8vo, 10*s*. 6*d*.

—— *Every-day English.* Crown 8vo, 10*s*. 6*d*.

—— *Studies in Shakespeare.* Crown 8vo, 10*s*. 6*d*.

White (R. Grant) Fate of Mansfield Humphreys, the Episode of Mr. Washington Adams in England, an Apology, &c. Crown 8vo, 6s.
—— *Words and their uses.* New Edit., crown 8vo, 10s. 6d.
Whittier (J. G.) The King's Missive, and later Poems. 18mo, choice parchment cover, 3s. 6d.
—— *The Whittier Birthday Book.* Extracts from the Author's writings, with Portrait and Illustrations. Uniform with the "Emerson Birthday Book." Square 16mo, very choice binding, 3s. 6d.
—— *Life of.* By R. A. UNDERWOOD. Cr. 8vo, cloth, 10s. 6d.
Williams (C. F.) Tariff Laws of the United States. 8vo, 10s. 6d.
Williams (H. W.) Diseases of the Eye. 8vo, 21s.
Wills, A Few Hints on Proving, without Professional Assistance. By a PROBATE COURT OFFICIAL. 8th Edition, revised, with Forms of Wills, Residuary Accounts, &c. Fcap. 8vo, cloth limp, 1s.
Wimbledon (Viscount) Life and Times, 1628-38. By C. DALTON. 2 vols., 8vo, 30s.
Witthaus (R. A.) Medical Student's Chemistry. 8vo, 16s.
Woodbury, History of Wood Engraving. Illustrated. 8vo, 18s.
Woolsey (C. D., LL.D.) Introduction to the Study of International Law. 5th Edition, demy 8vo, 18s.
Woolson (Constance F.) See "Low's Standard Novels."
Wright (H.) Friendship of God. Portrait, &c. Crown 8vo, 6s.
Written to Order; the Journeyings of an Irresponsible Egotist. Crown 8vo, 6s.

*Y*RIARTE *(Charles) Florence: its History.* Translated by C. B. PITMAN. Illustrated with 500 Engravings. Large imperial 4to, extra binding, gilt edges, 63s.; or 12 Parts, 5s. each.
History; the Medici; the Humanists; letters; arts; the Renaissance; illustrious Florentines; Etruscan art; monuments; sculpture; painting.

London:
SAMPSON LOW, MARSTON, SEARLE, & RIVINGTON,
CROWN BUILDINGS, 188, FLEET STREET, E.C.

www.ingramcontent.com/pod-product-compliance
Lightning Source LLC
Chambersburg PA
CBHW020816230426
43666CB00007B/1038